FOR CANDICE,

My Christmastime Baby

By Janice Monahan Rodgers

Letters To My Sister
Letters To My Sister, Volume 2

Available on Amazon.com

Text copyright © 2018 Janice Monahan Rodgers

All Rights Reserved. Except for use in any review, the reproduction or utilization of this work in whole or in part in any form by any electronic, mechanical or other means, now known or hereafter invented including Xerography, photocopying and recording or in any information storage or retrieval system is forbidden without the written permission of the publisher, Janice Monahan Rodgers.

Electronic edition published by Janice Monahan Rodgers

November 2018

Copyright © 2018 by Janice Monahan Rodgers

All rights reserved, including the right of reproduction, in whole or in part in any form. This book is a memoir. Some names, characters, places and incidents either are products of the author's imagination or are used fictitiously. Any resemblance to actual events locales, or persons living or dead is entirely coincidental.

TABLE OF CONTENTS

INTRODUCTION CHRISTMASES PAST

CHRISTMAS IS A 'COMING

CHRISTMAS IN JULY

TRICK OR TREAT

FRESH VERSUS FOWL

DAD'S NEW LOVE

LOSTED IN THE BUSTLE OF CHRISTMAS

THE WRONG TOY

TRIMMING THE TREE

AN UNEXPECTED GIFT

TALKING TO BABY JESUS

TWAS THE NIGHT BEFORE CHRISTMAS

ABOUT THE AUTHOR

Christmases Past

Memories of Christmas. Memories limned in gold. Memories of long ago. Yet, it's the little things we remember most about Christmas, isn't it?

For my sister, it was the advent calendar in the schoolroom marking down the days, the unique sugary taste of clear barley lollipops in toy shapes, the breathless anticipation that each day brought, the warm glow of electric candles in our windows filling our house with a golden radiance and lastly, the unbridled joy of a Christmas morning.

For my little brother, it was leading a covert maneuver to search any and all closets, snooping for presents. And the best undercover operation of all, getting up at three AM, along with his partners in crime, his sister and youngest brother, to steal downstairs and check out the gifts under the tree. (Probably had something to do with why he became a cop.)

For my husband, it was watching his mother paint a beautiful nativity scene on her front picture window with tempera paint. The first step in a week's long preparation to assemble the gigantic Christmas putz display that filled the front two rooms of his house. A magical village complete with trains, street lights, houses, churches and fluffy fake snow.

For my daughter Ann, it was poring through the Sears toy catalogue while making lists and leaving the list on the fireplace hearth addressed to Santa. Only to change her mind days later, leaving a revised list for the big guy. (Drove me, er, Santa Claus, nuts.)

For my daughter Candice, it was awakening to a bright movie light shining in her face as Daddy got ready to film surprised faces when she and her sister ran into the living room. Then, the sheer delight of seeing all those presents beneath the tree. And of course, the mystery of the plate of half eaten cookies and munched-on carrot sitting on the hearth, mingled with ashes from the grate, as though a great big elf had disturbed them.

Of course, for both my girls, an early December ritual was putting their shoes out the night before the feast of good St. Nicholas. On the morning of the sixth of December, those shoes would be filled with little treats, increasing their expectations for Christmas day.

For my brother-in-law, finding the bicycle he thought he would never get in his kitchen on Christmas morning was unforgettable. Not new, but better than new. Lovingly hand-painted and restored by his father. A gift that kept on giving, day after lovely day of freedom – his own wheels!

For my friend Mary, it was the trip out to the countryside to search for the perfect Christmas tree, eclipsed only by the mind-bending anticipation of waiting for her father to come home from work so they could put up the tree on Christmas Eve.

For my friend Del, it was seeing the toy ironing board and iron waiting under her Christmas tree. Now she could finally press her dollies' clothes. Her Christmas came a little early as she and her parents then journeyed to their parents' home town. A place filled with family who gathered to make ravioli and prepare a special fish dinner for Christmas Eve supper. And of course, the memory of the fresh baked bread she and her step grandfather secretly shared when no one was watching. Lathered with butter and toasted under the flames of the broiler, nothing could ever taste as good.

As for me, well for me it was and always will be, the smell of snow on the chill early December air, the still quiet before the snow fell, Christmas carols on the radio, the delectable aroma of Christmas cut-out cookies baking in the oven, and the glorious citrusy scent of a Douglas fir tree. If I close my eyes, I can still hear the whispering clickety-clack of my Lionel train racing around its oval track. Nor can I ever forget the thrumming joy of hearing our church choir singing Joy to the World as people left the church. Finally, the visit to the humble creche to talk to Baby Jesus before we embarked on a day of pure delight spent with friends and family.

As you can see, our Christmas memories are as diverse as we are. Perhaps, dear reader, your family celebrated on Christmas Eve instead of Christmas morning. Or maybe, like my friend,

Vicky, you were lucky enough to observe a traditional Christmas on the 25th and then Russian Christmas, which was celebrated on January 7th when legend promised, it would always snow.

Possibly your Christmases, like my friend Del, were spent traveling to be with grandparents, aunts, uncles, and cousins, anticipation building with every mile, until the joy of finally being with them filled your heart.

Christmas Is A 'Coming, gives the reader a peek through the misty window of memory into my family's past, the way we were in the 1950's and how we celebrated Christmas. It is surely a mirror of the times and lives of many other families as well.

Beginning with Halloween, right through to Christmas Eve, the tales echo a gentler time in our history. A time when baby dolls still said Mama, a red scooter was an excellent adventure, and a new jumping rope was every little girl's hope. When pearl handled cap pistols were every little cowboy's dream and a two wheeled bicycle was your ticket to the world.

In those days, Christmas time was a magical season when children's stockings might hold an orange and walnuts in their shells. Or, perhaps you received the little homespun box of Whitman's sampler chocolates. Maybe a tin of chocolate straws, or possibly red anise flavored candies found its way to your stash. If you were really lucky, there would be a box of chocolate covered cherry cordials, or ribbon candy with your gifts.

Whatever it was, however you celebrated, I hope my stories will help you recall those Christmases past that were filled with suspense, anticipation, hope, promise and love.

May the Christmas Babe share his light and love with you all.

Nollaig shona dhuit!   Vesele' Vianoce!
Merry Christmas!

CHRISTMAS IS A 'COMING

*Christmas is a 'coming,
and the goose is getting fat!
Please put a penny
in the old man's hat!
If you haven't got a penny,
A ha'penny will do
If you haven't got a ha'penny
Then God Bless you!*
English Children's Song

The voices of some older kids reciting this little ditty echoed in the street as they skipped by my house. I ran to the front window and pressed my face against the cold window pane just as they disappeared around the corner and down Railroad Street, their laughing and giggling still hanging in the icy air.

Even though I wasn't sure what it all meant, I liked the jingle. It was singsongy and fun. I tried singing it too.

Luckily, I didn't see too many old men walking around with hats, so I figured my pennies were safe, thank God. I had big plans for my current stash of cash at the candy counter of Reimer's grocery next door.

Nor was I worried about the goose part, since I wouldn't know a goose from a door knob. My Grammie only kept chickens when I lived with her.

But *Christmas is a 'coming!* Now there was a phrase filled with hope, promise and mystery.

It is 1945, and we have been in our *new* house for a few months. I noticed my parents have been *exceptionally* busy this past month, cleaning, moving things around, and going shopping. (Had I been more observant at that point, I would also have noticed a lot of furtive trips to the attic with packages.)

But I was just three and chalked up all the frenetic activity to my father's return from the war, moving into a new house, and a new job for Dad. We even had a new car parked out front. Well not quite new, but new enough for the three of us.

Certainly, ever since the war ended and Dad came home, there had been many changes in my young life. Not all of them great. For a three-year old, it was a lot of change to get used to. New house (small), new yard (tiny), new neighborhood (didn't know a soul), new church (very big) and lots of new neighbors (still strangers).

But now, with those kids running up and down the street chanting, it made me think. (They were older than me, so they probably knew stuff I didn't. Oh yeah, I figured this out at a tender age. Served me well all my life.)

So, maybe this "Christmas is a 'coming" thing they were singing about had more to do with all the recent hustle and bustle than I figured!

Christmas is a 'coming, I recited over and over! Now that seemed like something I could sink my teeth into. If kids were running around singing about it, it must be truly special, I figured.

I will note here that I have absolutely no memories of Christmas in my grandparent's house in Northampton where I lived the first three years of my life during the war years.

If we had a Christmas tree, I don't remember it at all. Were there presents? I couldn't tell you. Visit from Santa - not that I recall!

Perhaps it was because I was so young. But, oddly, I remember so many other events from those early years at Pop and Baba's house.

The smell of meals simmering on the coal cook stove, the taste of Mom's candied dates that she shared with me, slurping back a shot glass of cold beer on a hot summer's afternoon with Grandpop, and the warmth of a featherbed on a cold winter night.

But Christmas time - nothing. Nada. Zilch.

Of course, one might assume that while World War II was still raging, folks didn't feel much like celebrating. Gold stars were popping up all over town, and while their significance eluded me, the sadness that accompanied them did not.

No, for whatever reason, my Christmas memories began one cold December morning in a snug little row home on Chew Street, in Allentown, Pennsylvania.

I can hear my young Mother's still girlish voice calling to me. It is *very* early in the morning. (Even as a teeny child, I never did *early*!)

"Come on, Jannie. Get up. It's *Christmas*."

Christmas carols playing on the radio downstairs are softly tiptoeing up the stairs to my bedroom.

"Christmas? This is what those kids were singing about," I guessed. "Finally got here. But really, so early? They never mentioned that!"

Rubbing the sand from my eyes, I am magically transported downstairs to the *good* parlor at the front of our house. Still clad in my yellow Doctor Denton pj's, I can smell the heat coming through the floor grates. And something else. Something fresh, like the outside, like - *trees?*

There it is! In one corner of the room, my young father awaits, standing next to a huge fir tree adorned with red and blue see-through glass Christmas ornaments. Long, glittering strands of silver tinsel drape the tree's branches.

In a world still reeling from a world war, the clear glass balls are America's answer to war shortages. Made by Corning Glass Works and sold by the Shiny Brite Company, I think they are the most magical spheres I ever saw!

"Look, Jannie. Watch," Dad says, excitement coloring his voice.

With the flip of a switch, suddenly the tree and the front room is aglow with a million multi-color lights. I am dumbfounded, flabbergasted, astounded and pretty much amazed!

If I was half asleep before, I am fully awake now. Because the small parlor has just been transformed into a shimmering, rainbow-hued fairyland. It just keeps getting better.

Mom puts me down on the carpet and I gaze up at the tree in awe. It wasn't here last night. Did it just grow here? Overnight? Cool – if it did.

The citrusy aroma of pine fills the room. Gazing at the magic tree from top to bottom, I now notice a beautiful miniature Christmas village spread beneath it. Tiny houses covered in pretend snow dot the wintry landscape around a Christmas creche with Baby Jesus, Mary and Joseph who stands guard holding a lantern.

I am just getting used to the teeny Christmas village, when a shrill whistle grabs my attention. A sleek silver toy locomotive emerges from a pretend mountain tunnel behind the fir tree. It chugs around the oval train track with a whispery clickety-clack.

The Lionel train is hauling box cars, coal cars and a passenger car that is lit from within. There is a light in the engine too, probably so the tiny engineer can see, I assumed.

I lay down on my stomach to watch the train go 'round and 'round, hoping to catch a glimpse of the teeny engineer. If I look sharp, as my dad would say, I just might see him.

"Look what Santa brought you, honey."

Mom diverts my attention from the train and sitting back up on my knees, I notice something else. The room is filled with toys!

Santa brought this stuff? Oh yeah. The guy they took me to see at Hess Brothers. The old guy with the scraggly beard. Glory be. Who could forget him? Really, he looked like Father Time – on his way out! That beard! Scared the daylights out of me.

But I must say, scraggly beard or not, he did a great job here in my living room. It is pure magic. Enchanting, dreamlike, mystical, a fairytale.

A dolly in a glider swing sits next to a tea set. A little kitchen complete with sink and stove sits next to an airplane. Hold it! AN AIRPLANE? Yes, Ma'am. A B29, just like Dad flew in the war. It is silver, metal and huge! Bet that teeny train engineer could hop up on the smooth sleek wings and fly it. Cool! Way to go, Santa!

"Don't forget your stocking, Jannie." Mom grabs my attention once more and nods to the front door.

A red stocking with white stenciled Santa decorations, hangs on the front door knob. I pull it off and reach inside. An orange, a box of animal crackers, and Jujubes candies are stuffed inside.

I am overwhelmed. How did Santa know? My favorite stuff. I don't remember telling him that much. I was too terrified of him and his beard at the time.

My parents are standing, watching me with the silliest grins on their faces. They are positively giddy.

This is their first Christmas together since the war ended and our first Christmas as a family. It is 1945 and Sgt. Monahan has finally returned from the South Pacific.

This is my first true memory of a Christmas morning. It has never left me, has left its indelible imprint on my soul. All these years later, I can still see the glow of that front parlor, hear the whirr of that Lionel train, and smell that glorious pine tree.

I know, in my heart of hearts, that this is why each year at Christmastime, there will be a live tree in my parlor festooned with multi colored lights, glass ornaments and draped with tinsel. It is why a miniature village with teeny houses glistening with fake snow and a Christmas creche will lie beneath it.

It is why I will *not* look at my presents until Christmas morning, before I go to Mass. It is why there will be Christmas carols playing softly in the background.

For each of us, Christmas holds different memories or is celebrated in a variety of ways, observing all manner of customs.

My wish for you, dear reader, is that the child within you, still holds Christmas and all its wonders in your heart. May the Christmas Babe shine His light and blessings on you all!

Whatever it is, whatever it means to you, celebrate!

String those lights, bake those cookies, buy those gifts, sing those carols and put up that tree.

Because, *Christmas is a 'coming!*

CHRISTMAS IN JULY

> The dirty rats,
> they stole our sled!
> Give it right back,
> or you'll wish you were dead!

Now you may think that this is another one of those Christmasy, cheery, warming your toes by the fire, stories. Well hold onto your warming chestnuts, pal, because this ain't it. Oh no. The following is a tale of skullduggery, treachery, and betrayal. An account so vile, it will curl your toes. A saga so reprehensible, it will make you shudder. A narrative so unbelievable, it will strain credulity. A story searing with such duplicity, well, you get the picture.

But first, we must examine the players and our neighborhood dynamic at the time in order to understand this perfidious tale.

In our new neighborhood, back in the fifties, there was certainly no shortage of kids to play with. As we settled into our new surroundings, we got to know most of them.

We formed our neighborhood friendships, established clubs, and played all manner of games with our new buddies on a regular basis. Because we were now in the wide-open spaces of suburbia, games and playing outside took on a whole new connotation.

Tree houses were constructed and dismantled regularly, huts were built in fields, ball games were played in the empty lot across the street in the summer and the spring. In the winter, snow forts were constructed and sledding became a great competitive sport. We became all-weather kids.

Most of the time all was well and there were few arguments among us. Disagreements were settled promptly. Yes indeedy, it was Kumbaya, Lord, up and down the street. In the interest of solidarity, we all strived to get along.

That is why the sheer perfidy of my discovery on a hot sweltering July day, defies description. But this story actually begins on a rainy day in March when, apparently, I had nothing better to do.

"It's gone!" I announced heatedly to my mom.

"What's gone?" my mom said absently.

She was knee deep in making toll house cookies. Normally, I would have been right in there with her, but this morning I had bigger concerns.

"My sled, Mom. My sled's gone."

"What do you mean – gone?"

"Disappeared, vanished, eighty-sixed, thieved, nicked, the old five-fingered discount," I ranted.

"Really, Jannie, your language. You have to stop watching those old detective movies."

Language notwithstanding, my favorite three man (or two if some riders were, ahem, pudgy) was *missing.*

I loved that sled! It was a hand me down, but it flew like the wind, even if it wasn't all bright and shiny. Also, it was distinct. The steering handle had a little notch in it from the time I hit a cinder block and the steering bars had some red paint blotches were I once tried to sign my name with red nail polish.

Now it was gone!

"Just look around some more. Try the basement again. It might be behind something," Mom advised. "It's got to be around here somewhere. Or maybe Daddy put it out on the patio."

"It's not here, Mom," I said, whining. "And, I did look - everywhere. It's gone."

The unspoken 's' word circled our heads.

Mom looked out the kitchen window as torrents of rain slashed against it.

"Well, I don't think you're going to need it right now," she observed dryly, sliding a tin sheet of cookies into the oven.

"Yeah, I know, but I thought I'd paint it a little and…uh…"

"Do NOT go messing with paint now," she ordered, dropping a spoonful of cookie dough onto another tin sheet.

"Fine, but it's still missing," I said irritably.

Whenever I mentioned painting, my mom got crazy. Where I saw creative license, she saw a big fat mess.

"Now, Jannie, something that big just couldn't go off on its own. It's got to be around somewhere."

My mom was a sweet soul. For a cop's wife, she was so naive. She just could not conceive that it might have been nicked, thieved or - *stolen!*

Although, she was right on both counts. It *was* somewhere, and it didn't get there on its own!

As the rain hammered our suburban ranch house, I went on to other pursuits that day, and forgot about my sled.

Right up until around July.

It was a sweltering hot July day as I recall, and I was at loose ends. For a change, my chores were done, and Kathy, Jerry and Jimmy were otherwise occupied. (I believe they were engaged in yet another major construction project in one of the many vacant lots surrounding our neighborhood with the able assistance of the Fenstable twins.) So, I was on my own for a change. Free! Yay!

Musing about perhaps cleaning and organizing my closet, a sharp knock on the back screen-door brought me to me senses.

It was my friend Jilly.

"Hey, Jan. Are you busy?" Jilly asked.

"Not really. What's up?"

"Nothing. It's too hot to do much today."

"How about some iced tea? My mom just made some of that Bethlehem Steel recipe where you use a can of frozen lemonade," I suggested.

I really liked Jilly. She was a sweet girl and we got along well. She was only a year older than me, and we had a lot in common.

The aforementioned Fenstable twins, Carly and Billy, were her little brother and sister. They were just about the same ages as mine, so we could sympathize with one another. Particularly when our siblings were being annoying, which was just about every other day.

Especially *her* little brother and sister. I didn't think it possible, but those two actually made the Flynn brothers from my old neighborhood look saintly. At least with the Flynn's, you knew where you stood. Most of the time.

The Fenstable twins were another stripe entirely. For little kids, they had just about perfected the art of calculated resourcefulness. In short, you just couldn't trust what they were going to do next. Furtive could have been their middle name. Weasel also comes to mind.

But Jilly was a lovely girl. Nothing like those two, so I figured there was hope for them yet. If she could be so nice, surely, they would turn out ok.

Jilly and I sat on our glider swing on the patio sipping our iced tea and talking about the latest fan magazines, nail polish colors, jewelry, make up and movie stars.

"Hey, I just got some new movie magazines. Want to go over to my house?" Jilly asked.

"Sure."

Her mom was cleaning as we came in her kitchen door, so Jilly and I headed straight for her bedroom. As I happened to glance out her bedroom window, I could see Billy and Jimmy and Jerry working industriously on their fort. Kathy seemed deep in conversation with Carly.

Although, the more I looked, the more it looked like a 'discussion' was in progress. Perhaps a disagreement about the style of the structure was the problem? I hoped not.

Whatever, if they didn't settle it, we'd all know soon enough.

Kathy had a short fuse if she felt someone was trying to pull a fast one, and Jerry and Jimmy generally followed her lead. Mix in the twins' tricky personalities and you had a war.

Jilly opened her closet and rummaged around, extracting a bunch of movie magazines. We sat around on her bed reading and making comments like, I just love Audie Murphy, did you see his latest movie or I hate *her* new hair style.

"Come on, Jan. Let's take this stuff outside. It's too hot in here," Jilly said grabbing up the magazines.

As we started to walk through the kitchen, her mom stopped us.

"Sorry girls, you'll have to go out through the basement. "I just scrubbed the kitchen floor."

I thought I detected an odor of Pinesol. I was glad my mom didn't use it. I hated the smell of the stuff. For a nanosecond I mused on how our house smelled mostly like cookies. (That's probably because Mom was always baking. The four us cleaned out the cookie jar pretty darn quick.)

As we went down the stairs, I noticed that Jilly's basement was way bigger than ours, and it was stuffed to the rafters with all kinds of cellar type things. Tools, shovels, garden implements, buckets, old furniture, and it smelled of Pinesol too.

Hung on the walls were picture frames, garden hoses and assorted "we need to keep this stuff because we might need it later" things. Otherwise known as the detritus of living.

Although, for a basement, the place was bright and airy. Probably because it was a walk-out basement. There was lots of light and fresh air coming in the back door and it was wide open today.

We walked through a small hallway that led directly to the back yard. A few things were propped or hung against the wall and I scooted sideways to avoid the bikes, rakes and a sled.

Wait! Hold on! A SLED!

MY SLED!

Yes, a sled with the all too familiar notch in the top and the red paint on the steering bar. The scratched up, red painted initial "J" glared at me. If a sled could whine, this one would have.

"Where have you been?" it said. "I've been waiting here for months to go home."

My sled! It was here in my friend's basement, *the twins' basement*, all along.

"That's my sled," I blurted out.

"Are you sure?" Jilly gaped, obviously shocked.

"Sure, I'm sure. Look, here's my initial that I painted on the steering. Here's the notch I put in it."

First, I was stung by the discovery that after looking high and low for my sled, it was here all the time. Then, I was furious when I realized how it probably got here.

I knew Jilly didn't take it. She was just as surprised as I was.

No, the culprits, the twins, were only now walking up the embankment into the yard, followed by my siblings.

As a kid, I never, ever could come to grips with being blindsided. Still can't.

That is why the pure rottenness, the absolute betrayal of having a friend steal one of your things and then displaying it where you could see it, left me momentarily speechless.

Momentarily.

Ah, their sneakiness knew no bounds. These two could have given the Flynn Brothers lessons in duplicity. Oddly, for a cop's kid, I hadn't had too much contact with the criminal element. Until now. My Irish blood was boiling!

The light-fingered Louies (Billy and Carly) must have taken it back in March after the last snowfall.

"That's our sled," I growled as the twins walked up to me and Jilly.

"No, it's not," Billy nervously replied, his eyes shifting over to his twin. Aha, she of course was an accomplice, a willing participant in the crime. He wasn't a lawyer, so he didn't know that old axiom "possession is nine-tenths of the law." Tough, if he did. I wasn't budging without my sled.

"It's mine and I'm taking it - NOW!"

"I'm telling my mom," he said smirking.

"Good, go get her," I dared him.

He and his partner in crime took a powder into the house. While the little cowards beat a hasty retreat, Jilly helped me pull the sled off the rack on the wall. She knew it was ours but was caught in the middle and really didn't know what to say.

What could you say? It didn't matter, because *my* sled was going home with me, to *my* basement where it belonged. The two infantile delinquents returned as I hauled it out of the doorway. Their mother was conspicuously absent.

"Hey, what's our sled doing here?" Kathy asked as the rest of my troops crowded around the basement door. The face-off had begun!

But before a full-scale donnybrook could break out, the miscreants quickly retreated back into the safety of their own house. Probably to plan another heist.

That was how the clan M reclaimed their nicked, five-fingered discounted, stolen property.

We pulled our sled triumphantly through Manny M.'s yard in our very own impromptu *Christmas Parade,* while he watched and laughed at four kids hauling a sled around his vegetable patch on a hot July afternoon.

Victory was ours!

But remember that Kumbaya stuff? Well, several days later, peace was restored. The betrayal of the past forty-eight hours was *almost* forgotten, and everyone was chummy again. We chose not to harbor any grudges. (Actually, Mom chose not to for us.)

However, we did show the neighborhood that we weren't going to be pushovers. Sometimes you just have to stand up for what's yours and for what's right. Now, you might be saying, "Come on, it was just a sled."

Maybe, but it was mine! To me it had become a symbol of justice served. Long after the red paint chipped away and I put a few more notches in it, I just couldn't part with it. I kept that sled for many, many, many years. Never did paint it. Just kept it in clean condition and running order.

Over the years, my trusty sled and I coasted down many a hill packed with snow. As more years passed, my own children enjoyed the fun of sailing down snow-packed hills on it too.

In fact, even when I was much older and probably shouldn't have been sledding anyway, I glided down the hill in my backyard on it, enjoying every second of the ride.

I loved that sled.

Flew like the wind, it did!

TRICK OR TREAT

It was a dark and windy night. Somewhere up the street a dog barked. Blustery squalls sent dry leaves skittering around the back porch.

So, I figured this would be a good night to get into my pjs and read those movie magazines Aunt Ree gave me. I wanted to check out the one with Debbie Reynolds on the cover. Plus, I could work on my scrapbook too, since my homework was done.

"Jannie," my mom called as she came up the cellar steps.

"Jannie, you're taking Kathy and the boys trick or treating tonight," she promptly informed me.

I what, wait, no, I… ?

Trick or treating? No, no, no, no. In ten more days, I would be a teenager. Teenagers didn't go trick or treating.

"But, but, but," I sputtered.

My normally effusive smart-mouth retorts deserted me now in the face of this unexpected and unwelcome news.

"They're getting their costumes on now and they're so excited," my mom continued as she popped a basket of laundry onto the dining room table.

They have costumes, too? When did that happen? I really had to start paying more attention to what went on in my house.

Wait, costumes. That was it.

"Well *I* don't have a costume, Mom, so I can't possibly…"

My mom whipped a white sheet out of the basket and handed it to me.

Hold on! This was my own white sheet from my bed. The one with the red and blue flower trim that I liked so much. MY SHEET!

Gad, here I was, hoist with my own petard!

Great, just great. No way could I put holes for eyes in my favorite sheet. How the devil was I going to see where I was going?

Yeah, that was true. She just couldn't possibly send me out into the great unknown - blind?

"Mom, how am I going to see where I'm going?" I whined. "Besides, I still have home…"

"I know you finished your homework, Jannie," she cut me off. "You'll be just fine," she said taking the laundry into the bedroom.

This was awful. What kind of lame ghost prances around wearing a white sheet trimmed in red and blue flowers anyway?

Apparently, my kind, I thought as I walked out the front door surrounded by a fairy, a clown and a cowboy.

Adjusting my sheet until I looked like Julius Caesar, I began the recitation of the now famous Monahan orders which were delivered before every Monahan outing.

"Ok, now listen up! We're only going up to Union Street and then back," I instructed my motley crew. "That's far enough. And see that you all behave!" I said as another gust of wind threatened to strangle my words.

"Don't forget to say thank you," I barked into the wind as my charges took off at a clip.

First house, next door. Diamond's. Piece of cake. Mr. Diamond smiled and quietly gave us all candy.

One down, I thought.

Next house. Manny and Mary. Great neighbors, good friends, but Manny could be very uh, overenthusiastic, to say the least. In a word, he liked to tease. As a soon to be teenager, I was a little *sensitive.*

"If he says anything about my sheet, I'll kill him," I thought pulling my sheet over my face.

Ding Dong. Trick or Treat.

"Oh, don't you all look so cute," Mary gushed.

Manny stood behind her grinning from ear to ear. Even through my sheet, I just knew it. He didn't say a word.

Until I got to the curb, when he yelled, "You too, Jannie."

Gaah!

Actually, looking back over the years, this is the one and only time I ever remember going trick or treating. It was an unusual experience, to say the least!

Did we stop at a lot of houses? Yes, I guess we did.

Did we get a lot of candy? Oh, I am pretty sure we did.

Why is it then, that besides our two closest neighbors, I can only remember one other place we stopped? Vividly!

As we marched up the street, going from house to house, I figured I was way too cool to go trick or treating! The whole exercise was annoyingly painful for me. In my pre-teen prickliness, I felt the whole world was laughing at me.

Not to mention, each time we walked up to a house, I had to pull the dumb sheet over my head while articulating a muffled "triccortreat." Also, wearing a heavy winter jacket under my sheet, wrestling with my plastic pumpkin, and struggling to keep an eye on my three siblings, did not improve my disposition.

I didn't need candy that much!

As the winds blew and leaves flew, we worked our way up Leh Street, finally coming to a house that I had always admired.

Light spilled out from tall veranda-like windows that were framed by an ornate wrought iron porch. Between them, there were French doors looking out on a beautifully landscaped garden.

In today's world, we would call it charming. But, back then, to me, it was a mansion.

This was where the Macks lived - Mack as in huge car lot. Chamber of Commerce. Money.

As much as I wanted to get close to this house, I was scared stiff. These were wealthy people. Business people. Out of my league people. They might even be snobs. I'd heard about snobs, but didn't think I'd ever met any. Maybe we should give them a pass.

But while I was ruminating on this momentous decision, Kathy started prancing up to their door.

Ok, we'll just do our trick or treat repertoire, get our candy and split. Pronto.

Ding Dong.

"Trick or treat," the Monahan chorus sang - almost in harmony.

A well-dressed lady of about fifty stood in the doorway smiling. She was lovely. I figured it must be Mrs. Mack.

She was not quite what I expected. Medium height, well-coiffed hair, wearing a taffeta dress. No, not what I envisaged at all. Because, even in her stylish dress, she looked like a cookie-baking Grammy. Pleasant. Trusting. Kind.

Then this pleasant looking lady did the unthinkable! She invited all of us right in - into their house! No one else, in all the houses we visited, had done that.

Now I was shaking. We were going *into* the mansion. I was young enough to be suitably impressed by my surroundings and old enough to be suitably terrified by my surroundings. Suppose one of us tripped and we broke something. Oh God!

I looked at my fairy, clown and cowboy and started to pray. *Be good, don't dance around, don't jiggle, don't even breathe.*

Struggling with my sheet so I could actually see where I was going, I followed Mrs. Mack as she ushered us into a living room that was as big as our entire house.

It was, in a word, stunning. The living room was furnished with pieces of furniture like I'd never seen before. Two wing chairs and a plush sofa sat on one side of the room while book-filled shelves lined the other. Crystal and porcelain pieces were placed artfully on side tables around the room.

The long floor to ceiling windows were dressed with custom made drapes and matching valences. At the far end of the room, a beautiful staircase with a cherry rail rose to the second floor.

The whole room was warmly lit with several oriental style ceramic table lamps. Oddly though, as ornate as it was, the huge room had a cheery and homey feel.

I couldn't help but be in awe. I may have been only twelve, but I was impressed. I knew quality when I saw it.

Even my trick or treaters were awestruck, because for once they seemed to have temporarily lost their chattering mouths as they too gazed in awe around the room.

I was so busy gawking I didn't immediately notice the man seated in one of the wing chairs. Mr. Mack sat reading the newspaper and looked up with a warm, open look on his face, as though kids in costume regularly appeared in his lavish living room.

He was sort of a portly guy with thin, graying hair, and a great disarming smile. He chatted with all of us and didn't seemed to be the least perturbed at this intrusion into his quiet evening at home.

While Mr. Mack tried to engage us in conversation, Mrs. Mack went to get our treats. I remember standing there, sweating, aware that my hair was standing on end from pulling my sheet on and off so often, feeling distinctly uncomfortable. But my acute discomfort was about to get worse!
Because that's when movement on the stair landing caught my eye. I looked up and saw a movie-star gorgeous guy wearing a black turtleneck, slacks and corduroy sports jacket.

He looked like he just popped off the pages of my Silver Screen magazine.

He came down the steps part way and knelt down, leaning on the banister, to watch the proceedings. When he flashed his mega-watt smile at us, I became even more discomfited.

I may have only been twelve (well practically thirteen), but I recognized a dreamy guy when I saw one and I was sufficiently embarrassed to be standing in his living room, wrapped up like a mummy with several younger siblings in tow begging for candy. Gad!

As if that wasn't bad enough, a lovely blond suddenly appeared at the top of the stairs clad in a black slip, brushing her Rapunzel like blonde tresses.

Had I been a little older and more mature, I would have recognized this scene from any one of Tennessee William's plays.

"Oh, my, aren't you just the sweetest things. You all look so cute," the beautiful blond said and she really meant it. Her movie star companion agreed!

But cute wasn't what I would have called us. I did not feel cute! I felt self-conscious and nervous. I did not see what they saw.

Because, I guess we did present quite a picture. My siblings in their costumes, cheeks flushed from the warm room and me wrapped up like Julius Caesar ascending the Roman Senate stairs. We were lined up like half of the Trapp family, only we didn't sing as good as they did.

While Mrs. Mack doled out treats, I continued to wrestle with my sheet, all the while keeping a sharp eye on my charges, although truth be told, I wanted to keep looking at the gorgeous room (and the gorgeous guy on the staircase).

Finally, we said our politest 'thank yous' and then I carefully herded my pack out the front door! Once outside, I heaved a sigh and a 'thank you, God' that there were no mishaps. We headed into the wind for the next house.

I don't remember much after that except arriving home with enough candy and goodies to choke a horse.

Later that night, as I sat on my bed poring over my Silver Screen magazine, I thought about our experience at the Mack's impressive house.

The experience made me look around my own bedroom with fresh eyes.

The rose papered walls, and crisp white trim. The windows dressed in freshly pressed Priscilla curtains. The twin beds decorated with studded nail trim. The frilly boudoir lamps on my dresser that Mom won at bingo. The knick-knacks that came from Woolworth's.

It was a lovely room, cozy and snug. A soft rosy glow from the dresser lamps filled the shadowy corners.

Warm, comfortable, homey, just like the rest of our house, tiny though it may be.

I began to realize that it wasn't the expensive furnishings that made a house welcoming.

It was the people within.

As tiny and humble as our little house was, it was a special place because of my mother. She made it that way. She wanted all who entered within its walls to feel at home. She took pride in what she had, humble though it may have been. She taught us to take pride in what we had but to respect other's belongings as well.

The Mack house, with all its refined furnishings, had that same homey feel too.

I reflected on the difference between the two abodes. Two very different places; one refined and gracious and the other quite humble and modest. Yet both held an atmosphere of warmth and hospitality.

Sitting on my bed and munching gumdrops, I had kind of an epiphany. I began to realize that warmth and hospitality didn't come from how much money you had, but rather how you made people feel in your home.

Mrs. Mack had invited four little kids she didn't know into her home on a blustery October Halloween night, and she and her family made us feel welcome while we sheltered within its walls.

To my siblings and I, this in itself was a priceless gift. Better than all the candy in the world. Because I learned what true wealth really is.

The Mack's gracious house was homey and welcoming because of the pride they took in it and the love they brought to it.

So was our tiny abode, for the exact same reasons.

Pleased with myself and my profound observations, I popped another gumdrop into my mouth and returned to my Silver Screen magazine.

Guess I was growing up.

Thank you, Mom and the Mack Family, for giving me a lesson in generosity.

True wealth begins with a kind and generous spirit!

FRESH VERSUS FOWL

I stood outside the bathroom door and listened. Nothing. I put my ear up against the door. Couldn't hear a thing. Not a peep.

Hmm. I could always bang on the door.

No that wasn't a good idea. Mom would yell, if she heard me.

Maybe if I just jiggled the door handle a bit, it would elicit some sort of response. So, I tried a little jiggle.

Not a sound emanated from within the cavern that was our basement bathroom.

I tried looking through the keyhole. Couldn't see a thing. Just some gray light filtering in from the window above the toilet at the other end of the room.

Geez, what could *he* possibly be doing in there all this time? It was so quiet.

"Jannie," came my Mom's terse call. "Get up here right this minute."

"I'm comin'," I yelled as I high-tailed it up the cellar steps.

"What did I tell you about going down there?" she asked sharply.

"I just wanted to see," I whined.

"Never mind see. Go, go read a book," she ordered, and then turned to my father.

"Gerald, you have to get *him* out of there now. He just cannot stay in there any longer. What happens when one of *us* needs to use the bathroom?" she hissed quietly as though *he* could hear.

"I know, I know," Dad said in resignation. "Guess I'll call Harry. Maybe Harry will have an idea on how to get rid of *him*."

To think all this hullabaloo began the night before with a simple phone call. It went like this. Phone rings. Dad answers.

"Hello?"

Deep garbled sound.

"Oh, Hi, Lou. What's up, man?"

Then, more garbled noise on the phone which try as I might, I could not decipher.

"Yeah, I'm working nights. Why?"

Excited garbling.

"What? I won what?" Dad said, the excitement in his voice rising. "No kidding. I never win anything."

More garbled noise rises from the phone like bees buzzing.

"First prize? Well whaddya know." A big smile spreads across my father's countenance.

"Sure, you can drop it off. That'd be great," he says into the black receiver.

More garbled buzzing.

"Me neither. Geez, I just can't believe it. First prize, you say. Wait until I tell Marge."

Some garbled laughing and talking.

"No. She's at Bingo. She'll be shocked, because this time *I actually* won something."

Short garbled talking.

"See you tomorrow, Lou. And thanks." Dad hung up the receiver and strolled into the kitchen. Obviously, he wasn't telling *me* anything.

Wow, a major prize. I wondered what it could be. Something Mom would like, I bet. Jewelry maybe, or a new toaster. She'd like that.

But Dad was right about one thing. He never won anything. Well, there was that one time he bet on harness racing (also known as the sulky race) at the Allentown Fair, and his horse came in first place. He thought the guys were ribbing him when they told him he won, until they called him to the fair office to collect his winnings.

But whatever *this* prize was, we'd all have to wait until the next day to find out just what was coming.

Lordy, if we only knew!

The next morning dawned overcast and dampish cold. Typical pre-Thanksgiving weather in Pennsylvania.

Hallelujah, our major prize was due to be delivered anytime now, I figured.

I was getting antsy and dithering with my krispies. They weren't snapping or crackling as usual. My siblings, Jerry and Kathy were dithering too, which actually wasn't unusual for either of them, particularly Jerry. God, I never knew a kid who could take so long to eat.

Mom didn't seem too excited, so maybe Dad forgot to tell her about our imminent prize delivery. She's gonna be so surprised, I thought, smiling to myself.

Knock, knock, knock. The pounding on the front door interrupted my cereal dawdling.

I flipped the spoon aside and tried to beat Mom to the front door. She beat me by a mile. Good thing too!

BECAUSE…

She opened the front door and turned pale.

Then screamed bloody murder, "Oh. My. God. Gerraalldd!"

I peeked around her to see Officer Lou standing outside on our porch stoop with a big smile, struggling to hold a huge white, writhing mass of something.

Officer Lou, one of my Dad's police brothers, was short and stocky and seemed almost smothered by the thing he was carrying.

"Hi, Marge," he said wrestling with probably the biggest pile of feathers I've ever seen.

Meanwhile, Dad hotfooted it in from the kitchen.

"Margaret, what the heck." Only he didn't say heck.

"Here it is, Jerry," Officer Lou said with his signature mile-wide grin.

Dad's face suddenly had a blank look, kind of like he could not believe what his eyes were seeing.

"Geez, Lou, what the devil is that…I…"

"It's your prize. You know. Your first prize!" Lou spit out a few feathers.

"My prize?" Dad said like a sleepwalker awakening from a bad dream.

"Yeah, where do you want it?"

"Uh, I, uh, I guess we'll have to put it in the basement for now," Dad replied still in his sleepwalk mode.

I watched spellbound, as Officer Lou and Dad wrestled the thing past me and my cringing mother and into the basement.

As they went down the cellar steps, I heard an odd murkle, murkle, murkle sound.

What could make a sound like that, I wondered? Clearly, it was alive!

Cool. I always wanted a pet. But murkle, murkle, murkle. Didn't sound too promising to me.

Mom uncringed, sighed, turned on her heel and went back into the kitchen.

"Jannie, get in here and finish your breakfast," she ordered. "Stay out of the cellar."

My siblings were still working on their breakfast. Jerry now sported a wide milk mustache. Kathy was leaning out of her chair trying to see where Dad and Officer Lou went.

"Jannie, what was that?" Kathy asked, her eyes wide with curiosity.

Ah, apparently, she too heard the mysterious murkle, murkle, murkle.

Now in the world of sisterly relationships, this is where I could have had a bit of fun and really put the fear of God into Kathy by telling her all sorts of grisly things. But, I did not. Because, firstly, I didn't know too many grisly things to tell her. Secondly, Mom would for sure kill me.

So, I chose the high road. I simply replied, "Nothin'," and resumed my cereal dawdling.

A few minutes later I heard more muffled murkles and the bathroom door slamming as Dad and Officer Lou came clomping back up the cellar steps.

Dad escorted Officer Lou to the front door.

"Take it easy, Marge," Officer Lou called as he went out the door.

"Bye, Lou," Mom replied.

The door closed and everything got really, really quiet. Except for Jerry slurping his cereal. By now, he was sporting a triple milk mustache.

Dad walked slowly back into the kitchen. Slowly, like when you really don't want to go somewhere. Mom called it stalling.

"Honest to Pete, Marge," Dad said stalling his way into the kitchen. "I only bought the raffle ticket because they said it was a *fresh dressed turkey*."

"I don't care if he's wearing a tuxedo, you have to get him out of here," my mother commanded, hysteria rising in her normally placid voice.

A TURKEY! Really! We had a *live turkey* in our bathroom!

Now, dear reader, two very important things should be noted at this point. My mother was never fond of having live animals in her house. That's why we didn't even have a pet. She didn't like live fish, live chickens and don't even think about a pig. Also, she preferred her turkey fresh - but deceased!

The other thing was until that moment, I had no idea our bathroom guest was a *turkey*. The only turkeys I ever saw in my life were in a roasting pan surrounded by vegetables on Thanksgiving and Christmas.

Personally, I didn't see what the big deal was. Are you kidding me? I was probably the only kid in my neighborhood with a *live turkey* in their basement. That had to be a gigantic plus for my social standing among the neighborhood kids, probably for years.

Too bad Mom didn't want to keep him. I began to realize my golden opportunity to make a small fortune was about to fly the coop, so to speak. Why, with the right marketing, I could make a boatload of money. Let's see, charging a nickel a head to see the great white murkle beast would net me... Or on second thought, a dime was better. Oh yeah! Something this big was definitely worth a dime.

So, of course, whilst Mom and Dad discussed ways to dispatch the gobbler in the grotto, I snuck back down to the cellar to get a peek – at my money-making beast.

Alas, my plans were short lived when Mom called me back upstairs. The woman had eyes in the back of her head.

A few hours later Dad's other police brother knocked on our door. My siblings and I watched with curiosity as Officer Harry and Dad marched down to the cellar.

We heard a few more excited murkles from the basement bathroom and then nothing. All was quiet on the bathroom front.

A few minutes later, Dad and Harry, turkey wranglers extraordinaire, emerged from the basement with their quarry in a box.

Kathy, Jerry and I watched from the front window as our avian visitor was hauled out to Harry's waiting truck. Then the truck sped off into the great unknown, with our recent bathroom visitor's fate just as unknown.

Dad came back in and said, "Well, that's that," a satisfied look on his face.

He grabbed his jacket from the cellar landing coat closet.

"Marge, I'm taking a run out to the police home. Do you want anything while I'm out?"

"Yes. Don't forget to order a fresh turkey at the market while you're out," she called from the kitchen.

SAY WHAT?

HAPPY THANKSGIVING ALL!

DAD'S NEW LOVE

*And the night shall be filled with music,
and the cares that infest the day,
shall fold their tents, like the Arabs,
and as silently steal away.*
Longfellow

This is a tale of Dad's new love, or how a little blonde changed our lives forever.

Yes, it was all too true. Dad had a new love - a sleek, slim blonde. Very modern and 50's looking. Oddly, Mom didn't seem too worried or concerned.

But Dad had developed a magnificent obsession. Like most obsessions, this one seemed to escalate, *over-night.*

Mom began to grow just a tad concerned.

It began unobtrusively enough. You know, little gifts, *at first.* Hardly worth noticing. The special dusting cloths, a few record albums, a snazzy rack to fit them in. Then finally, the escalation, the piece de' resistance, *matching blond furniture.*

We all waited for Mom to say, "That's enough, Gerald." But, she never did.

Because Dad's new love was a sleek, modern Motorola Hi Fidelity floor model radio/record player (whew) - also known as Hi-Fi.

Hi Fidelity record players came in shortly after World War II and became increasingly popular with the masses. They stimulated the production of 33⅓ LPs (long playing records). The LPs really appealed to people like my Dad, whose tastes in music ran to classical pieces, because they could accommodate the entire classical piece, rather than just one selection.

Even better, the new record players had a tall spindle that allowed you to play a stack of records at one time, so you could have an hour or two of uninterrupted music. In the 1950's, this was *nirvana* to music lovers.

Now while I can't be sure what compelled Dad to purchase the floor model, I can make a fairly educated guess.

Recognizing his love and appreciation for good music, the prospect of putting on a stack of records, and then kicking back in an easy chair with a martini or two, must have been extremely appealing.

Add to this, the fact that he often worked extra jobs at local department stores as a store detective where he would have become acquainted with those stores' inventory – and *red tag sales* - and well, let's just say, he was doomed.

Normally a conservative man, he was not given to impulse purchases. So, I can just imagine the scenario when the siren-call of the little blond lured him ever closer to the shoals of financial peril.

What follows is my interpretation of one man's financial downfall.

It is early one fine Saturday morning and Allentown Detective Lieutenant Monahan is on duty at an extra job at Hess Brother's Department Store in Allentown.

It is the beginning of the Christmas shopping season, with turkey leftovers still holding sway on the top shelf of our refrigerator.

As he strolls through Floor Four, Fine Furniture and Rugs, not too much is going on. The floor is rather quiet today. But, it is still early.

After a swing through Appliances and Accessories, he will head to the loading docks and quietly have a look see. Folks had been known to walk off with TVs on their backs or a radio tucked under a jacket. He remembered the time he nabbed some guy who tried to walk off with a lawn mower from a Sears sale. I guess the culprit thought he could mow the sidewalk. Didn't work!

Later, Dad will assume his non-descript demeanor and meander around the first floor where the multitudes of shoppers would soon descend. (Looking ordinary was always a challenge for Dad. Tall and handsome, even in his worst clothes, he never quite fit the non-descript label.)

"Hi Jerry," says a salesman walking up to him.

"How's it going, Tommy?" he replies.

"Kind of quiet today," Tommy looks around the empty department, "but it's still early. Hey, Jerry, we just got some beautiful floor model record players in yesterday. Have you heard about that new stuff? They call it Hi-Fi."

"Sure, I've heard about them. Kind of pricey for my wallet though."

"Well there's no harm in looking, I always say, heh, heh," Tommy laughs cagily.

The two men saunter over to TVs and Small Appliances. Perched up against the wall, a saucy blond floor model Hi-Fi with slender legs reclines seductively with its enticing red sales tag prominently displayed.

"Isn't it a beauty, and wait 'til you hear the sound, Jerry! Why this High Fidelity, it's like nothing you ever heard before! Makes you feel like you're sitting right there with a full orchestra in your living room," Tommy raved.

Hey, it was a slow day, and thus far Dad was the only potential customer in the department.

"Let me show you this one. You've got some time, right?"

Before Dad can remind Tommy of his date with the loading dock, Tommy grabs his demo records and puts a stack on so he can demonstrate just how great this unit sounds.

The first record drops with a hushed plunk, the needle arm sweeps over and gently falls onto the record. An achingly sweet melody fills the air of TVs and Small Appliances, as the first selection plays. Rich notes swirl and eddy among the fryers, mixers and toasters.

Dad's face lights up. Oh yes, he can envision himself in his chair, martini in hand, as this pure, honeyed music pours over him, washing away the stains and cares of the day.

He is as entranced as a sailor hearing his first mermaid song.

Bingo! Tommy has just made his first sale of the day! He can take his kids to the movies tonight.

Several days later, the lovely blonde record player was delivered and placed in the dining room, flanking Mom's blonde dinette set.

"Oh, its lovely, Gerald," Mom cooed. "Look how nicely it matches the dining room set."

This alone made my mom happy because at least it didn't clash and it was soon enhanced by a matching blonde record cabinet.

Mom lost no time in making two crocheted doilies for the tops so the furniture wouldn't get scratched by careless passersby. (That would be us kids.)

Each payday I would wait to see what gift Dad would bring home for his new blonde friend. With a gleam in his eye, he would look positively gleeful as he came in the door from work and announced, "Look what I got today, kids!"

Waiting silently, we watched anxiously as the almost sacred ritual began. With the preciseness of a surgeon, he carefully removed the cellophane from his newest LP acquisition. Then, he would meticulously slide the record from its slip, gently place it on the spindle and turn on the player to a preset volume level. LOUD! (Dad always figured the neighbors' taste in music needed improvement.)

With a blaring crescendo, the strains of Mozart, Beethoven, Grieg or Tchaikovsky would build, filling the nooks and crannies of our little house on Leh Street. The rousing Hungarian dances, the Romanian Rhapsody or, occasionally, the light-footed pizzicato of the 'Humoresque' twirled around its tiny rooms.

(Every Saturday at dancing school, Mrs. Murphy played the Humoresque on the piano while we budding ballerinas pirouetted or leapt through the air. While I can no longer twirl, light-footed or otherwise, it's still one of my favorites.)

As time went on, our music appreciation increased, as we were introduced to Nelson Riddle, Roger Williams, and my personal favorite, Mantovani.

The addition of Dad's blonde friend to our humble abode certainly made a huge impact on everyone.

Mom would sing or hum along to the more modern classics as she ironed, and Kathy and I would swan around, ostensibly doing the dusting, while the lush notes of the Sleeping Beauty Ballet soared to the rafters. Why, even the boys got caught up in the William Tell Overture and galloped around the house, much to Mom's consternation.

Blondie's notes brought a new joy and vitality to our little family and changed the way we all viewed music.

Then, on one bitter cold December night, Dad came home late from work. He had been working an extra job for the holidays at, **wait for it**, *The Capitol Record Factory!*

I can still see him as he came in the front door on a blast of frigid air, face and ears red with the cold. Mom took one look at her frozen husband and went into the kitchen to make him a cup of tea.

Under his arm, he carried several record albums. *Boy oh boy*, he had that "wait until you hear this" gleam in his eye.

"Jannie, just look at what they gave me. You are going to love these."

He could barely contain his excitement. It was late and I was a trifle sleepy, but I always liked to wait up for him when he came home from work if Mom would let me. So sleepy or not, I caught his enthusiasm.

The sacred ritual began. Slowly, he removed the cellophane wrapper from the first album.

Gently, he pulled the record from its paper slip and placed it onto the spindle.

The album cover was beautiful. A snowy mountain top scene, with majestic, green fir trees, their branches bowing with pure white snow, that sparkled against a royal-blue sky. Emblazoned across the cover was the title *Christmas In Germany*.

The record dropped quietly onto the turntable as the two of us hunched over the Hi-Fi expectantly. We weren't disappointed.

Crystal-clear voices of a German kinder choir rose from the depths of Blondie's speakers as little children sang "Stille nacht, Heilige nacht."

Though they sang in German, I didn't need an interpreter to tell me what I was listening to.

The beautiful hymn, first performed at a Christmas Mass in Oberndorf, Austria in 1818, now arose from our little blonde friend. The timeless, classic carol composed by Father Joseph Mohr with melody by Franz Xavier Gruber filled our home and brought tears to our eyes.

Now, in 1955, Dad and I stood listening to one of the greatest gifts ever given to the world on that Christmas night so long ago.

Silent Night, Holy Night.

(Even now, almost 60 years later, I still have the album and copies of the CDs that I made. *Christmas in Germany* remains to this day my most favorite Christmas album of all time. One cannot listen to it without being transported to a snowy Bavarian village on a frosty, Christmas Eve. Indeed, for me, the holidays do not begin until I play it.)

On some weeknights, Dad would come home from work and plop a stack of Viennese waltzes on Blondie's spindle.

On a Saturday morning, Dad would rev up Blondie with John Philip Sousa blaring forth from its tiny speakers, daring us sleepyheads to remain in bed.

"Gerald, the neighbors," Mom would plead.

On Sunday mornings after Mass, Dad would come in the door, take off his hat and coat and put on a stack of records, while Mom and I started dinner.

Always, the house would be filled with music - entrancing, enchanting music.

It became a panacea for all our troubles. No matter how distressed we were, the spin of the turntable would soothe us, at least for a little while.

For every family gathering there was always some special music playing in the background to greet our relatives.

When Aunt Ree and Aunt Marie came to visit, the first thing Aunt Ree did was see what new selections she could put on Blondie's spindle.

When Aunt Polly and Uncle Bill and the cousins came to call, Hank Mancini, Nat King Cole or Arthur Fiedler and the Boston Pops were waiting to greet them.

Thanks to Blondie, family and friends were always treated to marvelous musical selections.

As the years passed, Blondie was finally replaced by the newer stereophonic sound and Dad's record collection grew to include classics, semi-classics, popular albums and some of the best Christmas albums I ever heard.

All of us kids came to recognize and enjoy a solid appreciation of all types of music - even if my siblings and I occasionally strayed.

Oh yes, it was inevitable. For as I entered my teens, my tastes had suddenly switched to a good-looking young singer, with a pouty mouth, swinging hips and a brassy guitar out of Tupelo, Mississippi. I am sure Dad despaired of me ever revering the classics again.

But while I had my flirtations with Elvis (The King), Pat Boone, Paul Anka and the Everly Brothers, I finally returned to my first love, and expanded my appreciation of all things classical.

Once upon a time, on a wintry Saturday afternoon, my dad made an impulse purchase in Hess's department store. What an extraordinarily, timeless Christmas gift it turned out to be. A gift of a lifetime of memories.

Inch by inch, record by record, Blondie had become a weaver - warping and wefting her musical threads, binding family and friends into a luxuriant tapestry.

The little floor model record player became intricately woven into our lives, spinning her magical musical moments over us all, binding us together for years to come. So that all these years later, the lush tapestry of musical memories could be unfurled at the first sound of a familiar tune.

It's Christmas again and I am transported back to that golden time. I can see my Aunt Ree standing in front of Blondie after putting another stack of records on the spindle. She is looking into the lens of my new Brownie super-flash camera.

"Smile, Aunt Ree", we yell and a bright flash captures this beautiful woman forever.

My gentle Aunt Marie is sitting in an armchair in the living room chatting with Dad and my little sister, Kathy. The boys, Jim and Jerry, are running around through the hallway as usual. Mom is in the kitchen, putting the final touches on dinner.

Aunt Polly and her family are now coming up our snow crusted walkway as the strains of the *Patapan* pour out the front door to greet them.

Thanks to Dad and his new love, magical golden memories of our family's life can be evoked just by the sound of a simple piece of music.

Well, excuse me now, I have really got to go. I want to listen to that new version of the Barcarolle, from the Tales of Hoffman. (It always reminds me of dancing around the house with my little sister on a Saturday afternoon.)

Dad would be so proud!

Now, just where the devil *did* I put my iPod?

LOSTED IN THE BUSTLE OF CHRISTMAS

*Christmas comes but once a year.
Now it's here, now it's here
Bringing lots of joy and cheer
Tra la, la, la la!*
S. Timberg, B. Rothberg, T. Seymour 1936

Screams rent the air. The ear-splitting crying of a child in dire distress bounced off the ceilings. They reverberated around the store full of Christmas shoppers while Christmas commerce ground to a halt.

It was pathetic. I literally froze in my spot, which was in front of the toy counter.

Ah, but wait one moment. I've gotten a little ahead of the story here.

Let's go back a tad, shall we?

We were, ah yes, singing of joy and cheer, now it's here, just like the little jingle at the top of this page says.

It was Christmas time. A period in our young lives, when my siblings and I planned lots of joy and cheer, tra la, la, la, la, beginning right around Thanksgiving Day, and up to and including the 25th of December.

But, goodness, while we had a ball, my poor mom. Well, let's just say, she worked tirelessly to make our holidays special.

The weeks preceding Christmas were always a frenzied time in our household just like many others, because they were chock full of Christmas preparations.

They began with non-stop baking sessions when the mouth-watering aroma of cookies, kiffles and nut rolls baking in the kitchen would swirl around every nook and cranny of our little row house on Chew Street.

Mom would always let us help her.

I wonder now at her patience with the four of us. It would have been so much easier, not to mention faster, without four small children mucking up the kitchen.

Our not so able assistance consisted of sprinkling sugar on cut-out cookies (and the floor, and us) and crushing walnuts with her old rolling pin for the nut rolls.

Also, since we didn't have a dog, broken and burned goodies were quickly dispatched by four hungry kids.

The kiffles, lekvar squares, cut-out cookies, nut and poppyseed rolls left cooling on our kitchen table were tantalizing. So, once they were completely cooled, all those goodies would be carefully whisked away to an undisclosed location in our house. Kind of like witness protection. Mom wasn't married to a cop for nothing!

Now, since the house was small, you would think we would have figured out where she stashed the stuff. Well, actually, I knew, but no way was I going to share sensitive information like that with my siblings! I knew when to keep my mouth shut.

I could be as silent as the grave, when it was necessary. I wasn't a cop's kid for nothing either.

After the baking, came the decorating. I remember we had those post-war red cellophane wreaths with a red electric candle in the center that we placed in our windows. End tables in the living room were populated with little choir boy candles. They lasted for years because they were never lit.

Of course, there was always the most wondrous, fragrant Douglas fir tree placed in the corner of the front parlor on a platform that Dad and his police buddies made.

We dressed Doug in the finest red and blue glass ornaments, silver tinsel and colored light strings. The Christmas putz beneath Doug was pure magic as our Lionel railroad train chugged past a snowy Christmas village and Christmas creche.

But in school, the nuns directing the Christmas pageant made sure our minds and hearts were focused on the real reason for all the holiday hubbub; the imminent arrival of Baby Jesus.

The few lucky enough to score a part in the show received grudging admiration from the rest of our classmates, thereby elevating our social standing considerably, particularly if you happened to be Joseph or Mary. The rest of us comprised the audience and allowed a giggle or two to slip out if one of the shepherds tripped on his robes or Mary dropped the Baby Jesus on his head.

Nor did our social life suffer during the pre-holiday season either, since Christmas parties flourished everywhere.

Each year my siblings and I eagerly awaited the big party at the Police Home. Once there, we could indulge in an afternoon of wolfing down hot dogs, birch beer, and candy. After playing games with our friends, we were entertained with movies and a visit from Santa bringing presents to all.

As the last day of school before Christmas vacation finally rolled around, precious little school work was accomplished amid the snacking and joyful anticipation of the Christmas holidays.

There was just one major drawback to this abundance of *fun and cheer*. We were supposed to be on our best behavior. *All the time.* Why you ask?

Because, Santa Claus was watching, that's why.

Apparently, he was omnipresent, kind of like God. He could see us when we slept and knew when we were awake too, the big fat spy. He even knew when we were good or bad! Imagine!

I mean, for goodness sakes. Life was tough enough for us kids back then. But being good for almost a month – well, come on. That was a near impossible task.

However, with the big pay-off (Christmas presents) approaching in our not too distant future, it was incentive enough. Most of the time.

But, occasionally, we had teeny setbacks. You know, like when we were supposed to do something and didn't or when we failed to fully grasp the seriousness of our responsibilities.

Since all of us in the Monahan household had our prescribed duties, (and I as the eldest had more than my younger siblings) it was bound to happen, of course. An error, a misstep, or an occasional slip-up in our daily comportment was inevitable.

Well, really, nobody's perfect. Keep this in mind, dear reader.

With a family of six, there really was an awful lot of work for Mom and Dad, too. Looking back now, I don't know how they managed everything. Financially or otherwise.

My mother had to be a fiscal mastermind to accomplish what she did with Dad's paycheck.

So, of course, when Christmas shopping reared its ugly head, Mom did it with all her children in tow. Paying for a babysitter was not even a consideration.

Which brings me to the crux of our tale, and how that being good and responsible rule almost got me into a barrel of trouble.

It was time to go Christmas shopping. That year I was nine, and my youngest brother was not yet born. So, Mom *only* had to contend with three of us, Kathy, Jerry and me. But when I think of it now, I marvel at her courage. She was a brave woman, taking the three of us actors uptown - on the trolley!

Once we were all suitably attired in leggings, coats, hats, scarves and mittens (whew) our little winter parade walked up the block to catch the trolley at Ridge Avenue.

As the eldest, and Mom's helper, I had been given explicit orders by her from the moment we debarked the trolley car on Hamilton Street.

"Now, Jannie, make sure you hold onto your sister's hand," her breath puffed like smoke into the chill December air, while she took hold of my brother. "And stay close to me."

"Uh huh," I answered grabbing my sister's hand.

Off we went, Mom with Jerry in tow and I, holding my little sister's hand.

It wasn't long, however, before I became distracted by the window displays in all the store fronts and the hectic pace of shoppers racing like lemmings to the sea of financial impoverishment.

There was movement and sound everywhere. Christmas carols blared forth from stores while the persistent ringing of a Salvation Army bell kept pace with crowds passing by.

Occasionally, the ringing would pause abruptly as coins were tossed into the black kettle. Of course, there was the ever-present clang and whir of trolley cars zipping along Hamilton Street, adding to the Christmas cacophony.

It was mind boggling, but I kept hold of my sister's hand and toddled close to Mom as we passed store after store.

One thing I should mention here, dear reader, was the fact that, like a lot of mother's, mine was perpetually afraid of losing one of her children. Understandable, since there *were* three of us by that time and we did tend to bounce around a lot. Hence, the holding hands and staying close rule.

Finally, we turned into Woolworth's five and ten cent store. It was a huge store and unique in that it had a basement as well, which offered clothing and housewares.

As we walked in the door, the mouth-watering aroma of pies, cakes and chocolate éclairs welcomed me. Along the wall on the right side of the store, was a lunch counter where they had the best blue-plate specials. I noticed chicken croquettes were on special today. They were my first choice when Mom and I stopped there for lunch.

My stomach rumbled at the mere thought of chicken croquettes swimming in chicken gravy with a side of chocolate éclairs. But today there wasn't time for lunch. We were on a mission. At least Mom was. The rest of us were just along for the ride, so to speak.

The store was sparkling with decorations everywhere. Glittering candy canes hung from the ceiling along with puffy red and green crepe paper bells. Everywhere you looked counters were piled high with all types of Christmas decorations and toys.

One counter had flocked Christmas trees of all sizes embedded in cotton batting. It looked like a snowy forest in the midst of mountains of toys. Another counter had puzzles, balls, games, crayons, coloring books and toy musical instruments while across from it was a display with every kind of doll you could ever want.

I was awestruck. There were toys everywhere. It was a veritable cornucopia of Christmas treasures. In spite of all the distractions though, all was going along swimmingly.

Mom made a small purchase at one counter and deftly hid it in her shopping bag. I tried to see what it was, but drat, she was too fast for me. Moving along, we stopped at another counter where yet another, bigger purchase was conducted and *zap*, into the shopping bag it went. Totally missed it again.

Ok, so now I had the hang of it. Mom was using stealth tactics. Resolving to be more aware, I watched carefully as we approached the next counter.

Meanwhile, however, unbeknownst to me, trouble was brewing in sister land. Kathy was getting restless and tried wriggling her tiny hand out of mine. My hand automatically tightened, and I pulled the two of us closer to the counter.

"Jannie, hold Jerry's hand for a minute," Mom ordered passing him to me.

I began to feel like a train, with Jerry on one side and Kathy on the other.

However, I kept watching as a covert conversation between my mom and the clerk ensued. Ah, apparently, a clandestine purchase of monumental proportion was about to be transacted.

I needed to be at the top of my game for this.

I did *not* need a wriggly little sister trying to break free of the hand that bound her.

"Kathy, hold my hand," I whispered trying not to miss the stealth operation going on in front of me.

But the little twit twisted and wriggled her hand even more. I grabbed her hand and squeezed harder trying not to miss what was going on with Mom and the clerk.

Something big was going down. Literally! Because the clerk was now on the floor behind the counter trying to wrap a ginormous package.

Standing on tiptoe, I thought I could just about make out a wooden peg sticking out of the bottom of the package.

Suddenly, I almost got jerked off my feet as Kathy twisted her hand and tried to pull away again.

"Givvve meee yourrr hand," I hissed through clenched teeth.

"I wanna see over there," she said pointing to the opposite side of the counter.

"We can't go over there. Just wait here and hold my hand."

"Nnoo," she insisted, trying to pull away.

"Give me your hand or else I'll tell Mom," I threatened, rapidly losing my patience.

"I just wanna see what's over there," she demanded trying to pull herself to the opposite side of the counter.

"No," I tartly replied.

But the lure of the unknown side of the counter, like the far side of the moon, was too much for my little sister.

She managed to wiggle free, Houdini-like, out of my grasp.

Fine, be that way, I thought and turned my attention to the more interesting proceedings in front of me, momentarily losing track of her.

But by now, the more than capable clerk, had just about finished wrapping our package in brown paper. Drat, missed it again, I thought.

For a moment I wondered what could possibly be in such an odd shaped package. More importantly, who was it for?

But just as the clerk began to lift the package over the counter, an ear-piercing scream split the air of the Woolworth's toy department, halting our purchase and pretty much everyone else's.

Ah, and this is where we came in, folks.

My poor mother was dumbfounded. She looked at me, her face a mask of confusion and then pure alarm.

"Where's Kathy?" she asked me, panic in her voice.

I looked beside me but she was gone, vanished into thin air.

Before I could formulate a response, another heart-rending wail rose from the other side of the counter.

"Mommmeee, I'm losssttted!"

A terrified child's voice filled the ether and mingled with cash registers jingling and the steady thrum of shoppers shopping. My little sister had wandered over to the other side of the wide, wonderful world of Woolworth's and found herself totally alone.

My mother quickly ran over and grabbed Kathy, hauling her safely back into the familial fold. Poor Mom. She was so embarrassed. She knew if my dad ever found out about this episode, there would be royal heck to pay. As a cop, he was always getting missing children reports and he sure didn't want one of them to be his own kid.

Kathy bawled for about two minutes and then order was restored.

I, however, was scared witless. For a brief time, a split second, I had allowed my curiosity to become my priority. That fast, she disappeared from my side. That fast!

It was all my fault. Guilt weighed heavy on my nine-year old chest, sending all thoughts of presents and chocolate éclairs flying.

Now in the overall scheme of things, this may seem like an insignificant event. But look closer. Isn't that how trouble oftentimes starts? With a minor problem.

I may have been only nine, but my careless lapse in judgement that day taught me plenty. Because, I knew, without being told, that it could have had disastrous results.

But God bless my mom, because I don't remember ever being reprimanded for my inattention that day. Apparently, she figured the whole event was lesson enough. Obviously, she was right, since I never forgot it. It did, however, teach me an invaluable lesson in responsibility.

When you are responsible for something or someone, you are also accountable. I realized that my mother really depended on me.

Was I too young to have all that on my nine-year old shoulders? Perhaps, but it was my duty. I never forgot it.

My sister was too young to grasp the folly of her actions that day. It was up to me, as the eldest, to know better.

So, that day long ago, in a Woolworth's five and ten cent store, I learned little sisters are more priceless than all the dolls, flocked Christmas trees or chocolate éclairs, even when they are being a pain in the…well, you know.

After all, I only have one.

Ah, but of course, you are still wondering, aren't you? You know you are.

What *was* in the package behind the counter?

Well, after my devastating experience with the sister that wouldn't stay put, I totally forgot about *the package*. Until Christmas morning.

There it was, set up beneath the tree, with the rest of my presents. Standing on long wooden peg legs, was an easel with a chalk board, two boxes of colored chalk and a felt eraser, just like in school.

The blackboard easel became a present that would allow me, as the eldest child, to teach my siblings about drawing, about numbers, about the alphabet, about love.

That Christmas, I stepped into my role as the big sister, and I never stepped out again.

THE WRONG TOY

Spring had sprung, summer was done, fall had fell, and Christmas was but a few weeks away.

This was the first Christmas in our new house on Leh Street. So, all of a sudden, there was so much to do and think about. Like, where to put the Christmas tree, where to hide our gifts, where to hang our stockings. You know, really important stuff.

Plus, Christmas vacation was rapidly approaching and, in a few days, we were going to go to the Police Home for the annual Christmas party. Something we eagerly looked forward to each year. In fact, we could barely contain ourselves and were constantly talking about it.

Apparently, while we rapturized about the hot dogs and birch beer we would have *and* the candy and presents we would get, our baby brother was taking mental note.

Actually, we *did* talk a lot about presents. There was all that speculation as to what we might get this year. Because, of course, the presents delivered by Santa were always extra special, we all agreed.

James listened.

"Do you think we'll get that good candy like we got last year?" Jerry asked.

"Probably," I replied, when I didn't have a clue. As eldest sister, however, my siblings pretty much took me at my word. Even if I was pulling some out of a hat.

But James was listening.

"I hope I get that dump truck I liked," Jerry said, while I envisioned another hole in the back yard.

James paid attention.

"Well, I'm asking for a paint set," Kathy added, her eyes lighting up with determination.

Ha. No way was that happening. I knew how my mother felt about us slopping around with paint. (That's why none of us ever became artists.) I also knew who Santa took his marching orders from. Mom ruled!

Trying to mollify my little sister though, I suggested tactfully that perhaps she should ask Santa for another gift.

"Yeah, well, if I were you, I'd ask for something else," I advised.

Kathy's face took on a thunderous expression.

"You know, just in case Santa runs out of paint sets. Wouldn't you like to have something like a Mrs. Potato Head?"

I needed to do some serious backpedaling before World War III broke out.

"Well, maybe a bake set," she thoughtfully conceded.

Whew, dodged a bullet on that one, I figured.

And James quietly observed.

So maybe we *older* siblings should bear some responsibility for what eventually happened. On second thought, nah. No way. I am *not* taking the wrap for what eventually transpired. Nope. Not happening!

For months, all Dad's buddies in the Police Department planned their annual Christmas party for their families which they held at the Police Home. When I say Police Home, however, you should note, this wasn't some lovely old mansion in the city. Not at all. The Police Home was an old stone and shingle bank barn in Lehigh Parkway situated amid rolling hills on what was obviously once a farm back in the day. Way back. Think horse and buggy.

The barn was cavernous, with huge beams and joists that soared high above our heads. It was a bit drafty, a little dusty, and very rustic. It was awesome. We kids, of course, loved it!

It had been somewhat renovated to accommodate social functions with the work being done mostly by the officers themselves. The first floor (or second if you entered from the rear) had a long bar in the corner with a mirror behind it. A huge brown wood stove for heat dominated an opposite wall and a small platform stage sat in the other corner for musicians or in this case – *the Christmas tree.* Also, the flooring was smooth like a huge dance floor, which we lost no time running and spinning around on, while the downstairs housed the kitchen and picnic tables for large dinners.

On their days off, the dads would work in teams, decorating the old barn with Christmas banners and of course, setting up the gigantic Christmas tree that stood on the corner platform. The beautiful tree filled the old barn with its piney perfume as it sparkled and glittered, and, to little kids, looked magical.

Even though the old stove in the corner kept the place warm, it was still a drafty barn, so Mom always made sure we dressed warmly, usually in flannel lined jeans and flannel shirts. The big day arrived, and we got dressed in our matching flannel shirts and jeans. (Yes, we all matched. That way Mom could pick us out in a crowd.) We grabbed our jackets and all piled into the car of the moment.

That year I think we were driving a dark green, two-door Chevy coupe. Room for three in the front and three in the back. Sitting in the back was a challenge though, since there was only the bottom half of a car seat to sit on and precious little leg room. (Riding in Dad's cars of the moment was always an adventure.)

When we reached the Police Home, chairs were already set up for us to watch movies and cartoons and any other entertainment the dads could round up for free.

This year, I was part of the free entertainment. I would perform my tap dance from my dance recital. My tap number was called Holiday for Strings, a wicked fast number that I wore out one pair of taps learning. I went to change into my costume, met my girlfriends who were also in the show, and we warmed up on the pseudo dance floor before our show started.

From a kid's point of view, we couldn't have had a better place to party. After all, how many kids get to run around a renovated barn, sit at a bar and drink birch beer while pretending they're tipsy, then twirl around a dance floor. Not too many, I'd bet.

Plus, the hot dogs and chips just kept coming. Downstairs in the kitchen, Officer Harry handed them out like candy. They were the absolute best. We were in heaven.

Especially my baby brother. I watched James running around with the other little kids, his face ruddy from excitement. The kid was having the time of his life. Burning the minutes until the big guy in the red suit made his appearance, bringing *Gifts*.

Finally, the big show started. One of the dads was the MC, another in charge of music and props and so on. They were actually pretty good at it. Either that or we were so stoked up on birch beer and candy that we didn't care if they missed a cue or not.

One good thing about performing for this bunch of little kids is they were all entranced by the costumes and music. Plus, we were the opening acts for Santa, so they were already in a very receptive frame of mind. Oh, and on their best behavior as well.

Anyway, we rocked our show. Our audience loved us!

But now that the opening acts were over, the mood began to shift in the decades old barn. A hushed, quiet air of expectation began to flow over the audience. An undercurrent of excitement ran just beneath it.

It was time. Time for the star to make his appearance. The major domo in the red suit. The big kahuna.

Now probably every kid in the place had already received several warnings from their parents. Be respectful and behave. Mind your manners when you speak to Santa. Don't forget to say thank you.

I know I heard it from mine. All four of us did. More than once.

But alas, one of our number (James) was not quite old enough to grasp the magnitude of the impending proceedings! Only God and Santa knew what he was thinking, surrounded as he was, by all that stimulation.

"Wait! Didja hear that?" one of his little pals said. The kid had to have ears like an elephant, because I heard nothing.

"No, what?" replied his companion.

"Bells, I heard bells."

A few seconds later I heard them too, coming from the direction of the lower level. The far-off jingle jangle of – sleigh bells. The jingle jangle got closer and louder.

Kids started squirming in their seats and looking all around. Including my little brother. This was it. The big moment. The Holy of Holies.

All of a sudden, HE appeared. Like Magic.

A crowd at the back of the room parted like the Red Sea and the big man stepped out. The red suited, white bearded totem himself! SANTA

CLAUS! Hauling a huge red bag full of gifts, just like all the stories said.

Santa proceeded to march up to the Christmas tree platform waving and Ho Ho Ho-ing to all as he passed. Kids were falling out of their seats (or standing on them) waving and yelling.

Now being cops kids, we all knew the penalties for disorderly conduct and a bit more about traffic control, so there was no mad rush. In fact, after the initial tumult of Santa's triumphant entry, we all lined up in orderly fashion, ably assisted by Officer Stan and Officer Ben, traffic duty cops.

While we stood in line and waited our turn to talk to the big guy and get our presents, it gave me some time to reflect and notice a few things.

Like Santa looked a tad familiar. In fact, he looked a lot like Officer Ralph, Dad's buddy and partner.

Officer Ralph was very jovial, a big guy, so I, at least, was pretty certain it was him. Santa seemed to have the same laughing eyes above his white beard. I don't think my siblings noticed since they were still rolling on birch beer, hot dogs and candy.

Certainly, from the awestruck expression on James' face, he didn't notice. To him, this was *Santa*.

The line moved along well enough, but apparently not fast enough for some kids. They were getting antsy. Anticipation will do that to you. It's called stress.

I watched my baby brother and I recognized that expression. Worry began to furrow his brows. Patience was never his strong suit, and he was still only three.

But finally, James stood in the august presence of Santa. The big man reached down and plopped James on his lap. A short (very short) conversation ensued. James, being a man of few words, said what he needed to say and tired of the wait, he took his present, said thanks, bounced off Santa's lap and took off.

Everywhere you looked, kids were ripping off wrappings and playing with their new toys. Laughter and squeals increased as the noise level of kids playing with their presents rang through the old barn's rafters.

I watched James sit down on the floor and proceed to demolish the wrappings of his present with mind boggling speed.

But who can understand the intricacies of a three-year old's mind?

Because, as he tore open his present, a look of sheer disappointment washed over his face. A look that rapidly turned to disgust. Uh oh.

James was not happy with his toy. I did not like the look on his face. It boded no good. For anyone in the vicinity. From my swift observation, that would be several of his pals, or (gasp) SANTA.

By now all the kids had received their presents and were otherwise occupied. The noise level had receded to an acceptable din.

Santa was basking in the glow of handing out free gifts to a hundred kids. Probably thinking about how good a nice cold birch beer would taste after all the ho ho ho-ing he did.

Now, at this point, had James been a truly thinking man, he would have heeded Mom and Dad's warnings to the four of us. You know, the aforementioned one about being good and minding our manners.

Also, the one about not ticking off Santa if one wishes to receive *future* presents. Ok, they didn't say that, but it was implicit in the song. You know, "You better watch out, you better not pout" and Holy Christmas presents, James was pouting big time.

For Pete's sake, this is the guy who sees you when you're sleeping, and who knows when you're awake and all that jazz. Mom had been singing that ditty to him for weeks.

However, James was just living "in the moment" so to speak. At just that *moment*, I watched a mega disaster begin to unfold.

James stood up, brushed off his flannel lined jeans and dropped his present on the floor. Jacked up on hot dogs, candy and birch beer, his intent was clear.

"Tell me he's not going to," I thought. He wouldn't – really? Assault and battery carry a stiff penalty in this state. Not to mention assaulting a legend.

Yet, unbelievably, I watched as James steamed over to the reposing Santa, with all the intent and purpose of a welter weight boxer entering the ring.

He stopped short in front of the big man. Then, yelling "YOU BIG FAT WAT!" at the top of his three-year old lungs, he took aim and kicked the legend, the icon, the Holy of Holies, right in the shins.

You could have heard a pin drop. Several pins in fact. Mom was crushed, Dad was mortified, and Ralph, er Santa, was flabbergasted.

After all, little kids the world over loved him. They were usually on their best behavior when they were getting presents from him. Generally speaking, they figured out that future presents depended on it. Apparently, James never got that memo.

Well, it didn't take long for Santa, er, Ralph to figure out what a 'wat' was! Ralph, er, Santa had all he could do to not lose it then and there. His face was as red as his suit.

After all what can you say to a three-year old who not only calls you fat, but a wat, er, rat too!

But Ralph was a good sport and took on his new moniker with the good cheer of the season, like the amiable man he always was. The 'fat wat' incident, as it came to be called, became sort of a legend of its own around the station house. A warning to future Santas.

As for James, well, then and there James earned the rep of a "Santa Claus kicker."

He never quite lived it down, either. For years thereafter, Ralph would occasionally remind James of the time he called Santa a "big fat wat". It never ceased to make Ralph laugh like the devil!

So, the phrase, once Dad got over the embarrassment (and that took years), became sort of a family battle cry for anyone who didn't quite measure up to the Monahan standards!

Why you, you, big fat wat!

Works for me!

FOR DAD, RALPH, HARRY, CHINKY, BOB, ERNIE, ARTIE, BOBBY, LOU, BILLY, GENE, JERRY, STAN, DICK, ADELE AND ALL THE OTHER OFFICERS IN BLUE WHO MADE OUR CHILDHOOD ABSOLUTELY WONDROUS.

GOD BLESS ALL OF YOU!

TRIMMING THE TREE

Oh Christmas tree, oh Christmas tree
Thy candles shine out brightly!
That makes each toy to sparkle bright,
Oh Christmas tree, oh Christmas tree, thy can-
dles shine out brightly!
Old English Folksong

The Christmas tree was out on the back porch.

Just waiting.

Kathy, Jerry, Jimmy and I sat around watching the clock.

Just waiting.

After a hectic day of cleaning and helping Mom bake, the last of the nut rolls were in the oven. Delicious aromas of the goodies as they baked, swirled through the house. We were on our best behavior. We did all our homework. We even ate our vegetables at dinner.

Did I mention we were on our best behavior?

(Trust me, knowing the clan Monahan, that bears repeating.)

But we were still, *just waiting*.

Any moment now, Dad would come home from work, bring in the Christmas tree and we could begin to put on the lights and decorations. We had carted the boxes of decorations up from the cellar so all would be in readiness for our great endeavor.

Christmas was always an exciting time for our family, and like kids the world over, the closer we got to the big day, the harder it became to contain ourselves. Decorating the tree and putting up the train and nativity scene would make us positively giddy with anticipation.

We were in such a thrall, we could even overlook the fact that Dad made us dust each glass ornament and place it perfectly on the tree. No problem, we declared. Even when he stood back and directed the placing of each strand of tinsel. No problem, we concurred. (Each silvery strand of tinsel had to be placed on the branches with military precision.)

"That's how the Marines do it," he would tell us.

So entranced were we by our mission, we never thought to ask him how often the United States Marines were mobilized to decorate Christmas trees. No matter. Nothing could quell our tree decorating enthusiasm.

But tonight, he was late. We all were getting antsy. Particularly Jerry, for some reason. Of the four of us kids, he always seemed to be the high energy, restless one.

Like most kids of the 50's, we assumed Christmas time was just a children's holiday. It was all about us. You know, a time of fun, Santa Claus, parties, presents, and good cheer.

We did not realize that adults had their own parties, sans kids! Parties that were overflowing with *plenty* of good cheer. With bubbles! Some that were intoxicating!

But right at that moment, we weren't thinking of Christmas parties. No, we were getting bored with waiting.

As sure as God made little green apples, our boredom would lead to something far worse. All that pent-up emotion and anxiety had to have an outlet. (You must understand that in our Irish Catholic family of four kids there was usually a perpetual state of war existing. Alliances were formed among us with alacrity and truces rarely lasted.)

If Dad didn't come home soon, there would be *war.* It was inevitable. We would start picking on one another. There would be a look, followed by a whine, followed by a smack. Followed by a return smack, and then it would *escalate.*

This would force the General (Mom) to use the divide and conquer strategy. We would all be sent to different corners of our house. (I would always opt for my room and not the basement.)

I watched as Jerry began to fidget and then started looking over at Jimmy and Kathy with that "wonder what would happen if I just belted one of them" look.

I sent a quick prayer heavenward for Dad to get a move on and come home, hoping that he didn't have to jail too many miscreants today. That would really gum up the tree trimming schedule.

Finally, as if in answer to my prayers, we heard the sound of a car pulling away and Dad coming up to the door.

Mom was in the kitchen checking the nut rolls, so I ran to open the door. (For some odd reason, Dad seemed to be having a wee bit of trouble fitting his key in the lock.)

I yanked the door open and he fell through the doorway with the silliest grin on his face that I have ever seen.

Jerry literally bounced off the sofa, followed by Jimmy.

"Hey Dad, you're home, you're finally home! Now we can decorate the tree," the two of them chorused at the top of their lungs.

Did I mention the two of them sang in the boys' choir at our church? It always amazed me that they could sit still that long. But their choirmaster, Father Della Picca, ran a tight ship. His mantra to rambunctious little boys was always, "Behave, else you get a smack!"

I watched as Dad *very* carefully walked over to the sofa.

He actually seemed to be having a little trouble remembering where it was. Once he located it (it was a small room), he plopped down on the sofa and pushed up his hat brim.

But then I noticed something I hadn't seen when he came in the door. His face was rather flushed. Probably because he still hadn't removed his coat, I figured. It *was* pretty cold out. But still, something was off.

I didn't have time to think about it because now Jerry was bouncing around the room like a ring-tailed monkey! His gymnastics were getting Jimmy all wound-up too.

God! Just what we needed, I thought. Someone, please get me a cage for these two.

"Dad, hey Dad," Jimmy jumped up on the sofa and sang in Dad's ear. I mean *in his ear.* He seemed to be having a little trouble getting Dad's attention.

"Can you bring in the tree now, Dad, huh, can you?" Jerry chanted.

"Yeah, we've been waiting all day," Jimmy added.

By this time, both Jerry and Jimmy, the Simian brothers, were bouncing on and off the sofa with excitement.

"Surrrre we can," Dad replied, slightly slurring his words.

I noticed then that Dad was starting to look a little green, kind of like the Christmas tree waiting on the back porch. I watched in fascination as his head fell onto his chest. He seemed to be studiously examining the carpet.

"But firsht," he announced, his head snapping back up as though he just remembered something vital, "we need to checkkk the lightsss."

His head promptly fell down again, whilst he studied that same something on the carpet.

Clearly, something was very wrong. With Dad. He was so, so distracted, I thought. He seemed to have wee bit of trouble concentrating.

So, being the eldest and most observant of his kids at that point, I called for help. Literally.

"Mommm," I yelled. "I don't think Dad's feeling too good."

Mom came into the living room from the kitchen, took one look at my nicely toasted father and ordered, "Gerald, get to bed right this minute."

"Oh nooo," he slurred. "We've got to check those light stringsss." He gave Mom a goofy grin.

Still bouncing back and forth on the sofa, the Jerry half of the simian twins said, "I'll get 'em for you, Dad!"

Suddenly, with the grace and purpose of a Polynesian pearl diver, he dove into the depths of the Christmas box, and swimming to the surface with his prize, reverently placed a mass of several tangled strings of Christmas lights into Dad's waiting hands.

Then, like the proverbial train wreck, things kind of went into slow motion!

The oven dings! The nut rolls are done.

"Gooo tooo beddd, Gerralddd," Mom orders and slowly turns to return to the kitchen.

Meanwhile, I watch the impending disaster unfold as Dad rolls the knot of tangled light strings over and over in his hands, mumbling something about a 'scrambled messss.'

He studies the entwined, knotty snarl like Einstein solving a relativity problem. Over and over, round and round he continues to examine the knotty mass. It was beginning to make me nauseous and I wasn't the one with a Christmas cheer problem. Suddenly his head pops up and the verdict is in.

"Theessse lightsss arre tangleddd."

"Buttt," he says and his head falls down again.

We wait with bated breath. Slowly his head rises. Dad seems to be having a bit of trouble focusing.

"Buttt, don'ttt chu worry. I cannn fixxx themmm," he slowly drawls, as the obvious solution hits him.

Abruptly, the fateful pronouncement is made.

"Gettt mee the scissorsssss!"

Faster than you can say, "Don't, Don't, For God's Sake Don't," Jerry turns and grabs the scissors that are conveniently sitting on the sofa end table with mom's crocheting.

He turns back and slaps them into Dad's outstretched palm, like a surgeon about to assist in a delicate surgery.

Oh my god! I thought. This is not going to end well!

"Do something, do something," my brain screamed!

But before I could get the words out, the snipping sound of Mom's scissors brings us crashing back to real time.

SNIP, SNIP, SNIP! Pieces of Christmas lights begin falling on the floor with a light thunk, as colored bulbs roll here and there.

Finally, I hear my own shattered voice screaming through the horrifying carnage unfolding before me. "Mommm! Dad's cutting up the Christmas lights."

A crash emanates from the kitchen as a cookie sheet full of nut rolls is slapped on top of the stove and Mom runs back into the living room.

"Oh, dear lord!" Mom gazes in shock at the chopped suey that was once our Christmas lights.

"That's it, Gerald," she yells. "Get to bed! Right - Now!"

Her normally tranquil voice is now quivering with shock and distress, in equal parts.

Dad wobbles off to bed and Mom returns to her nut rolls.

There is complete silence in the room. Even the simians are quiet – as I survey the now untangled but irreparably damaged Christmas lights.

Jimmy looks confused, Kathy looks ready to cry and Jerry starts to sniff, while I give them all a look that says, "Can it!"

Yes, fans, there was no joy in Monahanville that night! Mighty Monahan had struck out. Or snipped out, depending on how you look at it.

But with the resilience of youth, the next day the Christmas Light String debacle was completely forgotten (and forgiven) when Dad came home from work with boxes of brand-new Christmas tree lights, along with a new star for the tree top and some candy for us. (I'm certain it put quite a dent in his cigarette money allowance. Probably his lunch money too!)

Now, on the face of it, this story may seem like a rather insignificant tale today when light strings are so inexpensive. But back in the 50's, however, every penny in our household counted and we did not have money to burn. Electrically, smokingly or any otherly!

Later that night, the Christmas tree was hauled in from the back porch and placed in the corner of our modest living room. Decorated to the satisfaction of all, it sparkled with brand new lights. While a beautiful lighted star trimmed in red graced its tree top.

The 'cutting of the tree lights' disaster was not mentioned again - at least not until many years later when we *kids* were much older and could get away with ribbing Dad. He always took our kidding with grace and good humor when we reminded him of that December night's tragic event.

"Hey Dad, remember when you cut up all the Christmas tree lights?" we would tease.

I can still see him, laughing as he looked back through the years to that night so long ago. He would bow his head then and begin to chuckle at the memory of his four children watching wide-eyed while he solved the "tangled Christmas tree light problem."

So, dear reader, while this may seem like just a simple story of a guy who had a tad too much Christmas cheer one night, to my family, it is oh, so much more.

This is a story of a man who loved his children so much that he could not disappoint them. No matter what.

After all, he said he would fix the tree lights.

And he did!

AN UNEXPECTED GIFT

There's a holdup in the Bronx
Brooklyn's broken out in fights.
There's a traffic jam in Harlem
that's backed up to Jackson Heights.
There's a scout troop short a child
Khrushchev's due at Idlewild.....

Car 54, Where are you?
By Nat Hiken, John Strauss

Communication, consternation, exasperation, fascination, anticipation, irritation, resignation!

All these emotions and a few more were reflected on the faces of the Monahan clan as we stood in our family room and looked at the newest addition to its décor.

It was only three weeks until Christmas, and the last thing my mom needed to be saddled with in her lovely home where things had to blend, match or color coordinate, was this *eyesore*.

Consternation was written all over her face.

Dad was clearly irritated. But for the time being there was little he could do about it. His face reflected his irritability mixed with resignation.

My two younger brothers looked on our newest acquisition with a mixture of anticipation and fascination. Clearly, this could be a boon to them. Wait until their friends heard about it!

My sister and I, were clearly in the irritation camp. Just another thing to dust. Plus, it didn't match anything here in the family room.

The huge silver box with its dials and switches looked large, industrial and totally out of place in our cozy family room with its colorful afghans and recliner. The box rested on a small footstool, which was clearly too small and not sturdy enough to hold its weight.

"Well, it can't stay on this for long," Mom remarked testily, looking down at the wobbly footstool.

My normally placid Mother was not happy with this situation. Christmas was coming and so were visitors. Now there would be no place for a Christmas tree. The very last thing she needed was this contraption mucking up her Christmas décor.

"I guess maybe I can get one of the guys to build a cabinet for it," Dad said looking at the box with some derision. "Although, we'll probably have to put it over here in front of the windows. That seems to be the only place for it," Dad said, consternation compressing his lips. "For the time being," he added stoically.

The 'IT' was an ungainly, unsightly, metallic, silver, two-foot by four-foot, police radio receiver, and *it* was about to make a bigger impact on our family than we could possibly realize.

"Plug it in, Dad," Jimmy begged excitedly. The kid could barely contain himself.

"Yeah," Jerry echoed. Even though, as older brother, he wanted to show his 'cool', he was just as eager. "Let's hear what it sounds like."

Anticipation and fascination were reflected on both their faces like a Heinz ketchup commercial.

Dad plugged in the box and flipped the 'on' switch. Squawking, whistling and static like I never heard before, pierced the serene family room atmosphere. Gad, it made my teeth hurt.

Dad noodled around with the dials and the static and whistling actually got worse. So did the expression on Dad's face! It went from mild consternation to pure exasperation in record time. Dad *never* had patience with electronics.

Finally, after flipping more switches and turning dials, the radio settled down to a dull, annoying hum.

Then we heard it! A far-off, flat tonal, disembodied voice, crackled along the wires.

"Car four, car four – come in, car four."

Static "Car four here, Over."

"What's your twenty, car four - Over?"

"We're at fourth and s*tatic* street. Over."

"Ok, car four. We just got a call. Looks like a 10-23 in progress *static*, in your district. Proceed to *static* 42 *static* 5th street. Neighbors complaining. Some guys *static squawk* yelling *more static*, with an ax. Check it out! Over."

Squawk. "Roger, will do. On our way. Over and out."

"Holy cow!" Jimmy and Jerry looked at each other. "With an ax yet!" they both chorused. The two of them looked at each other as though they had just found the holy grail.

"Dad, what's a 10-23?" Jerry asked.

"Never mind," Dad answered irritably.

"Really, Gerald," Mom pleaded, "does that thing really have to be on all the time!"

Dad just gave her an exasperated look that spoke volumes.

But Mom could already see problems forming. She knew the boys' fascination with this thing was not going to be good.

How on earth was she going to watch her soaps on TV with this, this thing humming along right next to it?

Mom had made many sacrifices over the years being married to a policeman, but to give up *Search for Tomorrow*, now that was just asking too much!

However, my sister and I saw another impending crisis looming large on *our* teenage horizons.

What was going to happen when our girlfriends called and we wanted to talk PRIVATELY on the phone. Gad!

How positively mortifying! It would sound like we lived in a chicken coop, with all that squawking going on. Beyond embarrassing.

Now in order to understand how the beastly police radio came to be installed as part of the charming, homey décor in the Monahan family room, we need to remember a few changes that had recently taken place in our local municipal government at the time.

A new mayor by the name of Jack Gross had been elected. No stranger to municipal government, (Gross's father, Malcom, had been mayor for 16 years) one of Gross's top priorities was top flight law enforcement; a department peopled with the best officers, ready to meet any emergencies.

Mayor Gross lost no time naming his top two picks for the department. Chief Walter was appointed as his new chief and Gerald M., our dad, was promoted to Captain of Detectives. He would be second in command to the chief with all the authority that the position implied.

For a time, all this promotion business didn't involve us directly. Dad was busy being second in command. The department was changing, and communication was becoming a top priority.

What we didn't know at that moment was, that just days before Christmas, Dad would be named Deputy Chief, a position just created to improve coordination and management in the department.

So, the police radio (hereinafter referred to as the *Beast)* was transported to our home and installed in our family room as a further means of coordinating and managing.

This way, Dad (or Deputy Chief Monahan) could immediately be made aware of any trouble as it unfolded and could thereby contact headquarters to squelch any problems before they reached astronomic proportions.

Also, the Chief could reach Dad, should, God forbid, our phone line be busy. (Wish I had a nickel for all the times I heard, "Don't use the phone. I'm waiting for an important call.")

Lordy, talk about taking your work home with you!

The Beast took up residence squatting and squawking on the footstool like a demented parrot. But a week or two later the door-bell rang and two of Dad's police buddies appeared on our doorstep carrying a big wooden cabinet.

With a nod to the sleek lines of modern furniture (which who knew would one day make a comeback and be all the rage) the future lair of the Beast came equipped with sliding doors on the bottom to accommodate and hide unsightly storage and an opening on the top for the Beast to slide in and be somewhat concealed.

It was even stained a lovely cherry finish to match the paneling in the family room.

But frankly, fancy cabinet notwithstanding, there was not much you could do with the Beast to make it blend in. Clearly, it was the 800-pound gorilla in the room - and it spoke - noisily and often!

Now that it had a permanent home, it didn't take long for the boys to become enamored of the Beast's new digs. They sat glued to it for hours, waiting for a robbery or maybe a murder or any number of other grisly things to occur, their prurient interest being at an all-time high.

Fortunately, this being the late fifties, and Allentown being a relatively peaceful place, murder and other grisly crime was not exactly rampant, thank God.

But when the now familiar crackle started, the boys would drop whatever they were doing (dishes, homework, etc.) and would fly downstairs to the family room and wait expectantly for the transmission between dispatcher and car or foot patrolman to begin.

Of course, it was inevitable that the little dears would also pick up the dispatcher lingo and memorize the special codes used to describe the calls, in case somewhere the public might be listening (which we were).

Even Mom, succumbed to the lure of the beast and his static wiles.

For instance, if she was sitting there crocheting, and a call came over the bounding air waves with some urgency, say a 10-45 (accident), well, then *Search for Tomorrow* was momentarily forgotten as her attention focused on the Beast.

This would invariably cause her to drop a few stitches. I always knew when this happened because she would hiss and say something in Slovak while pulling out the recent stitch work on her current piece in progress.

Obviously, it was inevitable. It wasn't long before we all started talking like dispatchers and junior G-men. We kids would yell what's your 20 (are you in the basement or the bathroom) or, oh my god, it's a 10-35 (major crime alert), or did you hear about the 10-59 (burglary) at Hess's (this from my mother). Nor did we have to ask Dad "How was work today?" We pretty much knew.

Dad couldn't stand it. His home was supposed to be his place of rest and refuge. It wasn't enough that headquarters could call him on the phone at any time.

No. Now his home had become an extension of the squad room. He just wanted to come home and enjoy some peace and quiet, not to listen to more of what he just left. Worse yet, his kids were running around talking like a bunch of seasoned cops.

His favorite room had been invaded by the Beast. He wanted his refuge back and the beast out of his domicile.

We had been warned numerous times, not to speak of what we heard from 'the belly of the Beast'. This was police business, and not to be bandied about the neighborhood.

Oh yeah! Tell that to Jerry and Jimmy. Their stock among the neighborhood kids rose overnight.

Even Mom regaled the aunts with her new-found knowledge of all things criminal. You know, a hint, dropped subtly here and there at Bingo. A 10-4 or a 10-20 subtly interjected into a conversation. Just enough to feed curiosity and make her hints seem more enigmatic than they actually were.

My sister and I, however, could have cared less about the Beast. As long as it didn't interfere with our friend's phone calls and we didn't have to dust it too often, it was just another thing we would learn to live with.

Like Dad being called out in the dead of night, we would get used to it. Like the bullets in the ashtray on his dresser or his gun waiting in a locked box on the top shelf of the closet, it was part of Dad's job and our lives. Like watching him polish his brass shield and badge, the Beast was rapidly becoming a part of our home life and daily routine.

Christmas came and our tree was set up in the upstairs living room. Mom decorated the top of the Beast's lair with some Christmas candles and greens. Fancying it up with Christmas trimmings didn't change anything. It still looked like a Beast to me. Also, unlike a regular radio, it never played Christmas carols.

Even though the powers that be thought this was the greatest idea in communications since bottled beer, Dad clearly felt communication was best served with more modern methods. But he apparently decided to watch and wait and so the Beast remained.

Dad was nothing, if not a good soldier.

The days and weeks passed. Dad took to reading upstairs in the living room and avoided his recliner. Certain rules were put in place.

Homework was to be done upstairs in the bedroom or kitchen, not in the family room! No entertaining neighbor kids with the Beast crackling.

If the Beast called out to us in its plaintive, mesmerizing static, we were to ignore it. Dad probably hoped it would short out or self-combust or whatever. No such luck, even with my Dad's electronically challenged ministrations.

Some calls were clearly not meant to be heard by children or teenagers either. They were harsh, sad, pitiful, rotten and often depressing, emanating from a world Dad and Mom had always tried their best to shield us from. Now, in this dawn of burgeoning communications, here it was, being piped into their own home.

I quietly began to wonder how much longer it would be before the administration and the Big 'G' (Dad) had a showdown over the Beast.

As a recent graduate of the FBI academy in Washington, DC and Quantico, Virginia, Dad longed to put more modern methods of communication into the hands of his fellow officers.

He wanted his officers to have instant contact in addition to the police Gamewell call-in boxes. He could envision a communications system upgrade with repeater system stations. With policemen needing to be in constant contact, he wanted foot patrolmen armed with the newer Handi-Talkies, so they could communicate more rapidly when they needed help.

For now, though, he had to bide his time and enthusiasm. But you know, sometimes the good soldiers, those who do their job, those who watch and wait, are rewarded.

Christmas had long since passed, but another would soon be upon us. So, I figured there would be no tree in the family room again.

Instead Mom planned to put a lighted ceramic tree on top of the Beast's lair. It had held sway over the family room for months, but was losing its allure. At least, as far as I was concerned. To me, it was still just a clunky radio.

Then late one fall evening as we sat around our family room watching TV with the Beast crackling in the background, the phone rang.

Ah, it was the Mayor. From the brief, muffled conversation I tried to overhear (in spite of the crackling irritant), Dad had been summoned to the Mayor's home on the qt.

Hmm. "Wonder what's up," I thought fleetingly. "What's the big mystery?"

I really didn't pay too much attention. Mom didn't seem too interested either and just kept on crocheting while Dad grabbed his jacket, said his goodbyes and left.

Probably just another problem in the city, I figured. Guess we'll find out all about it in the morning papers.

Several days after his clandestine meeting at the Mayor's home, we *did* find out all about it along with many other Allentonians.

The Chief had accepted a new post with the state department. And, Dad had been appointed the 29th Police Chief in the City of Allentown.

Of course, we were all beyond proud. This was big stuff. Our dad was now the new Police Chief. How cool was that!

The good soldier had finally been rewarded.

One of the first things the born leader and good soldier did as the new chief was to institute a few changes of his own.

Yes, the Beast was finally transported out of the family room and into his office downtown in the police building where it belonged.

Now his officers had Handi-Talkies, and a new communications system was in progress. Soon there would be training programs and his dream, a Police Academy, would eventually be realized.

Even better, he could finally sit in his recliner and watch the Monday night fights with Howard Cosell and a martini without the crackling static of another Monday night fight in progress on Sixth Street.

As for our latest furniture acquisition, the Beast's lair was quickly transformed into a lovely bookcase. Mom even got to put her new ceramic Christmas tree on top of it a few weeks later. With the Beast now removed, the cabinet actually looked pretty nice decorated for Christmas.

But more importantly, though, for my family, we actually did receive an unexpected Christmas present in the guise of an irritating police radio.

Because, during that window of time while the department went through its growing pains, my family got a peek into the real, everyday world of the police officer. The annoying crackling Beast with its myriad calls, helped us understand Dad's job and have more respect for what he and his police brothers had to sustain.

The calls were at times exciting, sad, exhilarating, treacherous and grave. We learned to appreciate the dangers these men and women faced each and every day, sometimes from the most innocuous sources.

Years later, when Mom finally got new furniture, the book case was relegated to the basement from whence I rescued it and gave it a new coat of paint and a new home.

The Beast's lair now stands in my kitchen, a reminder of a long- ago time when two men's visions for the future began to coalesce but fate intervened and set them on divergent paths that allowed them to use the talents to which they were born.

TALKING TO BABY JESUS

Christmas Morning   1944

The hushed murmurs of people, the scent of incense and candles burning, the flickering banks of votive candles, the citrusy piney smell of Christmas trees encircling a little house on the altar, the softly uttered prayers as people prayed for their loved ones, prayed for the war to end, prayed for peace.

Svata Maria, Matka Bozia, they intoned in Slovak. 'Holy Mary, Mother of God'.

It is December 25th, 1944 and I hear my Mother softly utter my Father's name in her prayers at the altar. I sense the murmurs of the congregation and smell pine trees mingled with incense. This is my only recollection of Christmas morning in Blessed Virgin Church. It is barely a memory, but marks the beginning of my annual visits to the Christmas Babe.

Christmas Morning   1945

Good parents will do almost anything for their children. Mine certainly did. I was now three-years old and had already figured that out. But I was about to learn not everything in life was that simple. Not everyone could afford a good roof over their head or food on their table or heat in their house. Hence, I should be grateful for what I had.

It was Christmas morning and I stood with my parents before the nativity scene in Immaculate Conception Church, on Ridge Avenue in Allentown, Pennsylvania.

The altar smelled of incense, candlewax and pine trees. It was decked out in its most beautiful Christmas finery for the Holy Family. A wrought iron stand of red votive candles cast flickering shadows on the creche.

My mother leaned down and whispered, "Jannie you can talk to Baby Jesus and He will hear you. Tell Him anything. He will always listen."

But looking at the rickety stable and manger before me, it was hard for me to comprehend what I was seeing. There he was, Baby Jesus, wrapped up in what looked like white kitchen towels (and not too much else), laying in a manger on a bed of hay.

You'd think that a Supreme Being in charge of the whole world would have had a better crib for his only kid, I thought, as I stared down at this Babe.

I know Mom told me earlier that this was just a copy of where He was born and he lived in Heaven now, but still, it was a rough looking house to start out in. Even I could figure that out.

Glancing at the stable roof, it looked pretty shabby to me. Kind of like Grandpop's chicken coop, only with moss all over it. That angel perched on the top isn't doing that roof much good either, I figured. And really, laying a teeny baby like that on hay! I played in hay at my friends' Grammy's farm in the summer and I can tell you, hay isn't soft. It's itchy, plus it makes you sneeze.

Looking down at the manger and the happy baby statue face I decided to talk to Baby Jesus, knowing He would hear me where ever he lived now. My mom would never lie.

"I sure hope you get a better house soon," I whispered to the little Babe. "And maybe a nice warm pair of pj's like mine." I thought of how nice my yellow Doctor Denton's would look on Him. My Mother took my hand and we lit a candle beside the Christmas nativity scene. "See you next year," I waved.

Christmas Morning 1946

The nativity scene was surrounded with Christmas trees decorated with colored lights. Baby Jesus pretty much looked the same as last year and his roof hadn't improved either. But at least it hadn't collapsed. Still dripping with dried-out moss, though.

Dad and I joined the line of people slowly shuffling up the aisle, waiting to pray to Baby Jesus.

I was anxious to get up to the front of the altar because I had a lot to thank Him for this year.

"Thanks, Baby Jesus for all my gifts. I know you probably told Santa where I lived. Oh, and thanks for the baby sister, too. She's pretty small to play games with yet, and Mom said not to try feeding her any more potato chips. I figured she'd like them, but I guess she needs more teeth."

"I see you still have the same house," I whispered, giving the humble barn a critical once over. "Well, maybe they can at least fix the roof. See you next year."

Christmas Morning   1947

Cold and snowy just the way Christmas should be, I thought looking out our front window. It was still flurrying. I squirmed and jammed my foot into my Goodyear rubber boots for the walk up to our church on Ridge Avenue. I really wanted to stay home and play with my new toys, but I knew Baby Jesus was waiting. I hated to disappoint Him.

The church was warm and toasty when we walked in. I could smell the dusty heat coming out of the radiators. Mom blessed me with holy water like she always did since I couldn't reach the font. Up front on the right side of the altar, Baby Jesus waited.

"Oh Baby Jesus, I got a beautiful doll house for Christmas this morning. You'd love it. It has a bathroom, and a kitchen with a teeny sink and a living room with a sofa and bedroom with a crib and a, a…". I looked at the Baby Jesus statue face smiling back at me from the manger. He never had a crib. In fact, He was still living in the same stable, basically. And the roof looked worse than last year. "I'll say a prayer for Father Mike to fix your roof. I hope your house in Heaven is nicer than this. Maybe it's nice like my doll house. Thank you for all my blessings this past year – and the doll house too. See you next year."

Christmas Morning   1949

It was a frosty Christmas morning as we walked the few blocks up Ridge Avenue. But inside Immaculate Conception Church, the altar glowed warmly with candles surrounded by Christmas flowers.

During mass, the choir and parishioners sang my favorite Christmas carols, including the Harold angels one. Then we got to do one of my favorite things of Christmas. Praying to Baby Jesus at the nativity scene. Everything was quiet, even my little sister. She looked like she was enjoying the red votive candles. Dad lit our candles and then we moved to the creche.

"Hi Baby Jesus. Thanks for getting Santa to my house with all the neat toys and stuff. I got the cutest tea set. I'm making my First Holy Communion soon. I know the Act of Contrition by heart now. And Mom's getting me a white dress. I can hardly wait. By the way, thanks for the baby brother too, but it's getting a little crowded with him *and* a sister too. Plus, he does a lot of crying." I looked over the rude stable and whispered, "But I guess we're better off than you. We'd never all fit in here. Hope you get a new house soon. See you next year."

Christmas Morning   1950

"Now remember, Jannie, only wind it eight times. Don't overwind it," Aunt Kitty cautioned me.

"Really, Kitty, she's much too young for a wrist watch," my mom protested.

My Aunt Kitty was always showing up with great presents and for my birthday a few weeks before Christmas she presented me with a Bulova ladies wrist watch.

So naturally, I had to wear it this Christmas morning. I needed to show it to Baby Jesus.

"Thanks Baby Jesus for all my blessings, and for all the nice presents Santa brought. And please bless my Aunt Kitty for the beautiful watch she gave me," I said extending my skinny arm. "Also, I promised in school to pray for the pagan babies. So please take care of them, where ever they are. Oh, and my little sister and baby brother too. They're not pagans, but they could use your care too. Good to see you finally got some new moss on your stable roof.

Looks nice. Merry Christmas. See you next year."

Christmas Morning   1952

Christmas morning and the altar is glowing with candles. Even the arch lights are lit. Because, of course, it's a special occasion. The whole place smells like a forest with all the pine trees on the altar. Everything seems new and beautiful this year. I love my church. The marble floors, the dark pews, and especially all the saints and clouds that are painted on the ceiling. Dad and I kneel by the nativity scene, and I look down at the Babe in swaddling clothes.

"Happy Birthday, Baby Jesus. Thanks for all the neat presents. I know it was all you and not Santa Claus. I love the new sweater. And the gold vanity mirror set looks so nice on my dresser. Please take care of my Mom, because soon we're going to have a new baby brother or sister. I do try to help Mom with the *other two*. Mom's talking about a new house, but she says it will be awhile yet. Speaking of houses, I noticed they finally fixed your roof. You got a new angel too. About time. See you next year."

Christmas Morning   1953

This church is sooo different. St. Catharine's is beautiful in a plain, modern way. And brand new. It still has that brand-new, just built smell. And it's so bright and light. Very different from Immaculate Conception with its darker, hallowed feel.

The parishioners here outgrew the church in the first floor of the school building long ago. I never did enjoy going to Mass in there because it was so crowded.

But I miss Immaculate Conception Church with its frescoed painted ceilings, stained glass windows and gothic arches. I used to love looking up at those ceilings as the angels and saints floating up there watched over me.

St. Catherine's ceilings are just – high and white. One thing hasn't changed though, I notice, as I kneel down to pray.

"Happy Birthday, Baby Jesus. Thanks for getting me through the past few months. It was harder than I thought moving here. I miss my friends from my old school, but I met some nice girls in the school-yard, Del and Mary. They seem very nice. I hope they like me. Some of the other girls seem to already have their own friends though, and I feel so out of place. Things are so different here. Like you can't go home for lunch. They have a cafeteria. And the school bus ride in the morning is very, very long, not to mention noisy. Some of the kids on the bus are a real pain, especially Donald. One girl is pretty nice though and she invited me to her house next week. Her name is Vitalia, I think. It's an odd name, but pretty, like her. I hope she likes me. Guess I shouldn't complain, though. I notice your house here isn't any better than it was at Immaculate. Some fresh moss couldn't hurt. See you next year."

Christmas Morning   1956

Everyone piled into the car, with Mom urging Dad to hurry. Because, as usual, Dad's always the last one. He's also the driver, so we are not going anywhere without him. It's really cold out there this Christmas morning. Glad I got this new coat. It's gorgeous. But I really need to have a chat with Baby Jesus after Mass.

"Happy Birthday, Baby Jesus. Thank you for all my gifts of the past year and for keeping me safe. I'm in high school now. It's not too bad. I have good friends from grade school with me, and I'm making even more pals. The nuns are a little stern, but I guess they have to be. Especially Sister Eufrida. For a short, little nun, she scares the devil out of me. Perhaps that's the point. I was kind of nervous about changing class rooms, but I think I finally figured out where I'm going and how to get there. It's a pretty big school and we have to move through three buildings. No crossing over in the hallway either. If you don't follow the traffic pattern you could end up with a detention. Dad would kill me.

"Thanks too for keeping my Dad safe while he was in Washington and Virginia. Even though we missed him while he was away, we were so proud when he graduated from the FBI Academy. He worked so hard."

"I see you still have the same humble home. Good to know I can always count on you to remain the same and keep me humble too. See you next year."

Christmas Morning   1959

St. Catherine's looks beautiful this morning. Just brimming with color. There must be two hundred poinsettias on the altar and dazzling candles everywhere. The vivid red flowers look fantastic against the austere marble altar. Word is that St. Catherine's is going to become a cathedral. Maybe they'll snazzy it up a bit. I wouldn't mind a bit more bling. But of course, one thing remains unchanged. I kneel down in front of the nativity scene.

"Happy Birthday, Baby Jesus. My, it's been a busy year. In a few short months, I'll be graduating high school. Thank you for all those late-night chats, and getting me through mid-term exams. Especially chemistry. What was I thinking? I should have taken Home Ec. Well maybe somewhere down the road, I'll go to college. I don't know what's in store for me yet, but I do know you'll be a big part of my life, my choices. Help me to make the right ones."

"I see you're still in the same stable. I guess after 1900 years or so, you've kind of gotten used to it. But, you know, a new angel couldn't hurt. Maybe some fresh moss on the roof. A couple of new slats in the wall. Did I tell you I really love you, BJ? I do. See you next year."

Present Day

Many Christmases have come and gone since my first remembrance of standing before the creche. Then there was a terrible war raging and so many fathers, sons and brothers were missing from the small town of Northampton. It was a time when people gathered together often to hold vigils for their boys, or to hold drives for paper, rubber, metal and anything else the war effort demanded.

The one thing I will always remember, albeit hazily, is the murmur of the people chanting the Hail Mary in Slovak that Christmas Day so long ago. In churches all around the little cement town of Northampton, the community held tight to the hope that soon, soon, the war would end, and everything would be right once again.

Now my world is much, much older, but hardly any the wiser. The Christmas Babe has heard me speak of more wars; Korea, Vietnam, Desert Storm, Afghanistan, Iraq and one we only called *Cold.*

Over the years I have spoken often to Baby Jesus. He has measured my successes, helped me accept disappointments, guided my steps around a murky morass of despair and self-doubt and been my rock in times of heartbreak and tragedy.

So, I will continue to talk to the Baby Jesus. To let him know how I am faring, to thank Him for all my blessings, to plead with Him to keep me and mine safe and to bring all of us His blessed peace.

Remember, you can tell Him anything and He will always listen.

My Mom told me so!

TWAS THE NIGHT BEFORE CHRISTMAS

Twas the night before Christmas,
And all through the house,
Not a creature was stirring,
Except…

My younger siblings, Kathy and Jerry, who were planning a Christmas Eve stake-out.

Being cops kids, they actually knew the meaning of the word, since they saw our dad leaving for stake-outs many times. Now for the uninformed, a stake-out in police parlance, means lying in wait for a criminal, watching and waiting for his arrival so as to observe his movements in order to prove a crime will, or is about to occur. In other words, secret surveillance to observe a perp's activities. With the desired objective of catching the perp in the act.

In this case, it wasn't exactly a crime they were concerned with, but the breaking and entering perp himself. SANTA CLAUS!

Now where were we. Ah, yes.

Twas the night before Christmas – in our humble house. The stockings were hung on the doorknobs with care, in hopes that St. Nicholas soon would be there, when we kids were all shooed up the stair – to bed.

Baby brother was asleep, but Kathy and Jerry had been planning their middle of the night foray all day. It was fairly evident from the whispering, furtive conversations, shifty looks and the rummaging around the house the two of them engaged in for the better part of the day.

But on this special night, by bedtime, even more mischief was afoot. Literally. The two miscreants ran back and forth between the bedrooms alternately laughing and whispering.

Personally, I didn't have time for their nonsense. It was Christmas Eve, for heaven's sake. I was tired. And not just a little anxious to see what Santa brought *me* in the morning. IN THE MORNING! Which meant it was time to get "nestled in our beds".

"You two better settle down and get to sleep," I called from my room. "You know, Mom and Dad can hear you downstairs. It probably sounds like a herd of wild elephants running around up here," I warned them.

They both stopped bouncing and giggling. Clearly, they had not considered this. If they were planning something, (and they were) they needed to reconsider their tactics, to practice more - *stealth*.

I heard muted whispering and then the boinging of bedsprings as the two of them jumped into their beds.

"Ok, we're in bed now, Jannie," Kathy called sweetly. Ha. Like sugar wouldn't melt in her mouth.

"Great," I answered. "Now just shut up and go to sleep." I rolled over in my bed intending to do just that.

At long last, the children were nestled all snug in their beds, waiting for visions of sugar plums to dance in their heads. Well, at least it was quiet from their end of the house.

Downstairs in the front parlor, the Christmas tree, trimmed in its finery, glistened in the darkness.

The sound of steady breathing soon emanated from my siblings' room, proving that they were finally nestled snuggly and sleeping.

It wasn't too long after, the stairs creaked as Mom and Dad prepared to settle their brains for a long winters' nap.

The hour grew late, and the house grew still.

Not a creature was stirring. Not even a mouse. (Because we didn't have any. Mom would have freaked.)

I lay in my bed thinking of sugar plums. Wonder what sugar plums are really. Hmm, plums dipped in sugar. That sounded pretty good actually. Or Sugared plums, or just plums or... plums with....

I drifted off. Dreaming, dreaming, of that plum colored sweater I saw at Hess Brothers department store.

Sleeping. Dreaming. Snoring.

When suddenly from the foot of my bed there arose a boinging clatter. I sprang up in my bed to see what was the matter.

Hit my head on the headboard and saw stars like a flash, because somebody actually was *shining* a flash-light in my eyes. Two somebody's actually.

When what to my watering eyes should appear, but a wide-awake little sister and little brother too.

I knew in a moment, it wasn't St. Nick.

It was the stake-out duo.

When did the little darlings get Dad's flashlight, I wondered, shielding my sleep deprived eyes. The next thing I know, they'll be toting around his black jack. Now there's a chilling prospect.

I shivered at the thought of the two of them swinging the heavy weighted leather nightstick.

"What are you two doing out of bed?" I whispered, loudly. "Mom and Dad will have a conniption fit if they catch you. You need to get back to bed. Right now!"

"Aww. Come on, Jan. We're going downstairs to see if Santa came yet," Kathy whispered back at me.

"Yeah," added her partner in crime solving. "Maybe we can catch *him*." Jerry waved Dad's flashlight around almost blinding me.

A look at my clock said quarter to three.

"Are you kidding me? It's the middle of the night!"

At the ripe old age of ten, I knew Santa Claus was now happily sawing zzz's in the front bedroom dreaming of his own sugar plums after assembling myriad toys. Mrs. Claus was doing the same.

As for myself, I had long passed the infantile stage where I needed to find out what Santa brought me or snooped around the house looking for signs of presents.

In fact, for my idea of a perfect Christmas, it was of paramount importance that I see my presents displayed beneath the tree on Christmas morning. MORNING. Long after Santa and his coursers came – and went.

Ok, so technically, you could argue it was three AM and now morning. But no, no, no. I didn't want to see anything until like around six or seven when Mom and Dad called us downstairs.

Another thing to note here is that Mom and Dad or Santa didn't wrap anything. Our gifts were displayed beneath the tree, where the jolly old elf placed them before he sprang to his sleigh and dashed away, dashed away, dashed away all.

Wrecked the whole Christmas thing for me to know what I got ahead of time.

My siblings, apparently, had not yet learned this invaluable lesson.

"Jannie, aren't you excited? Don't you want to see what's there?" Jerry asked.

"No, I do not. And I'm not going down yet, so DO NOT tell me what I got - or else!"

I lay back pulling the covers up to my eyes.

"Ok, but we're going to check it out," Kathy said sliding off the bed.

Their rustling and furtive movements made nary a clatter, as they slid from my bed to see what was the matter. Away to the staircase they flew like a flash…unlocked the baby gate and slipped down to inspect their stash.

Really, the two of them could have made a bundle as cat burglars. For cops' kids, they knew a little too much about covert operations.

Like Dasher, and Dancer, the vixens, they came, at the top of the staircase, they called out my name.

"Come on, Jannie."

"Absolutely not," I hissed.

And then in a twinkling, I heard on the stairs, the prancing and pawing of two little pairs – of feet. Down to the living room the two of them flew, to check on their toys and St. Nicholas too.

They spoke not a word, but went straight to their work.

With a sleigh full of toys crammed under our tree, I heard from beneath a winding toy key. Then, a mama doll crying, a police car whirring, a thump, some toy dishes clinking, and the bells on their stockings jingling.

Holy Christmas presents. They've gone through everything, the brats. They better not touch my stuff. Or I'll smack them silly. Christmas or not.

I rolled over and tried to settle. Even ten-year old girls needed their beauty sleep.

As I drew in my hands and was turning around, up the stairs Jerry came with a bound, plopping down on my bed with more than one sound.

His eyes, (what I could see in the flashlight glow), how they twinkled, his cheeks flushed like cherries, as he leaned over and I detected the fruity smell of Jujyfruits candy on his breath.

Curling up beside me, he calmly ticked off the presents Santa brought him.

"And wait till you see what you got, Jannie. There's a…".

"SHHSH. Don't you dare say another word!" I hissed.

"But don't you wanna know," he said chewing his candy. Smelled like lemon and raspberry.

"I do not!"

"Ok then," he said. A blink of his eyes and a twist of his tow head, soon gave me to know I had nothing more to dread.

Then as dry leaves that before the wild hurricane fly, when they meet with an obstacle, mount to the sky, off the bed, to the stair top he flew.

And giving his team a short whistle, flew back down the stairs like the down of a thistle.

Minutes later, the successful stake-out complete, the two stealthily climbed back up the stairs, whispering of their feat.

They spoke not a word then, but went straight to their beds.

But I heard them exclaim ere they dove out of sight,

"Merry Christmas, Jannie! Guess what! You got a …"

I covered my head with a pillow and sang Jingle Bells.

With my sincerest apologies
to Clement Moore

Merry Christmas To All and
To All A Good Night!

ABOUT THE AUTHOR

Janice Monahan Rodgers lives in Northampton, Pennsylvania with her husband and one finicky rescued tuxedo cat. She has two lovely daughters and enjoys writing for children. You can contact her via email,
jmrodgersauthor@gmail.com
or visit her website at https://janicemonahanrodgers.com/

Christmas Is A 'Coming is her third book of short stories. Besides personal memoirs, Mrs. Rodgers also has several children's books in process, targeted for 2019 publication. Look for *The Red Cape Caper*, first book in *The Circus Mysteries* series, a children's chapter book, soon.

Made in the
USA
Middletown, DE